LIVING & WORKING ONBOARD

CHAPMAN

LIVING &
WORKING
ONBOARD

DAVE KELLEY

HEARST BOOKS
A DIVISION OF STERLING PUBLISHING CO., INC.
NEW YORK

Copyright © 2004 by Hearst Books.

All rights reserved. The written instructions and illustrations in this volume are intended for the personal use of the reader and may be reproduced for that purpose only. Any other use, especially commercial use, is forbidden under law without the written permission of the copyright holder.

Library of Congress Cataloging-in-Publication Data

Kelley, Dave.
Chapman living & working onboard / by Dave Kelley.
p. cm.
Includes index.
ISBN 1-58816-321-0
1. Boat living. 2. Quality of life. 3. Quality of work life. 4. Boats and boating. I. Title: Chapman living and working onboard. II. Title.

GV777.7.K45 2004
797.1--dc22   2003056852

10 9 8 7 6 5 4 3 2 1

CHAPMAN and **CHAPMAN PILOTING** and **Hearst Books** are trademarks owned by **Hearst Communications, Inc.**

For specific references, boaters should refer to manufacturers' or suppliers' written instructions. In any event, the publisher and the author are not responsible for any errors or omissions contained herein, nor for loss or injury of any kind, including property damage, personal injury, or any actual, special, incidental, contingent or consequential damages of any kind. The publisher and the author are not responsible for the availability, safety, or quality of products, methods, or services of any kind.

PRODUCED BY
J.A. Ball Associates, Inc., and designlabnyc
Jacqueline A. Ball, *Producer*
Andrew Willett, *Editor*

Todd Cooper, *Creative Director*
Sonia Gauba, *Designer*
Jay Jaffe, *Designer*
Brian Herzig, *Production*

PUBLISHED BY
Hearst Books
A Division of Sterling Publishing Co., Inc.
387 Park Avenue South, New York, N.Y. 10016

Distributed in Canada by Sterling Publishing
c/o Canadian Manda Group, One Atlantic Avenue, Suite 105
Toronto, Ontario, Canada M6K 3E7

Printed in China

ISBN 1-58816-321-0

To Mom and Dad for their unwavering
support, and to Carey, with whom I'd live
and work anywhere.

CONTENTS

▶ Chapter One
Making the Decision 9

▶ Chapter Two
Choosing a Boat 23

▶ Chapter Three
Choosing a Home Port 51

▶ Chapter Four
Setting Up the Office 59

▶ Chapter Five
Adjusting to Life Onboard 83

▶ Chapter Six
Safety and Seamanship 107

▶ Chapter Seven
Special Challenges 131

▶ Chapter Eight
Togetherness 143

▶ Chapter Nine
Charting Your Own Course 157

Acknowledgments/ Photography Credits 172

Resources 173

Index 174

CHAPTER 1

MAKING THE DECISION

IT'S SAFE TO SAY THAT AT SOME POINT VIRTUALLY EVERYONE WHO'S EVER OWNED A BOAT HAS ENTERTAINED THE NOTION OF SAYING "ADIOS" TO THE LANDLUBBING LIFE AND MOVING ONTO THE BOAT FULL TIME. HARDLY ANY OF US ACTUALLY DO THIS, OF COURSE, BECAUSE IT'S PRETTY TOUGH TO SHUCK NORMAL LIFE ALTOGETHER. BUT THANKS TO THE ADVENT OF WIRELESS TECHNOLOGY AND EMPLOYERS WHO ARE WILLING TO LET THEIR STAFF WORK AT REMOTE LOCALES, MORE AND MORE OF US ARE TURNING OUR BOATS INTO THE ULTIMATE VACATION HOME, WHERE WE CAN LIVE, PLAY, AND WORK FOR A WEEK, A MONTH, A SUMMER, OR EVEN A YEAR.

I'm willing to bet that the vast majority of the people who make the decision to live and work onboard even for a short time start out spending just a weekend

CONTENTS

▶ Onboard Benefits

▶ Know Your Limits

▶ Know Your Boat

▶ Consider the Family

The dream of trading in a landlocked existence for life onboard is increasingly attainable, thanks to technology and more flexible workplace rules.

or so on their boats, discover they can actually pull this off, and then start spending longer and longer periods onboard. The change occurs gradually, so that you might not even notice it until you're completely hooked. That first weekend goes so well that you schedule another, and the next thing you know you're spending just about every weekend out on the water. Then you start getting a little cocky. You sneak out for a day in the middle of the week, telling your boss you're "working from home," but you're really out on the water with a cell phone close at hand, checking your voice mail every fifteen minutes. And now you're hooked.

There's more to it than that. You can, after all, take off and work remotely from campsites, RV parks, the middle of the Mojave desert, the rest areas alongside the Interstate, your mom's house, or even the golf course if you have a mind to. But a boat's different. A boat gives you the opportunity to cleanse yourself psychically and spiritually because it puts you on the water. Henry David Thoreau retreated to the woods of Walden but wound up by the pond, if you remember, and Paul Gauguin was just another unknown French painter until he set his easel up on the beaches of Tahiti.

Orcas, a.k.a. new neighbors to some Pacific Northwest liveaboards.

Sooke Harbour House at Sooke Harbour, Vancouver Island: a fine place to get away from it all.

THE GETAWAY

Of course, you don't have to leave civilization behind completely to get the benefits. I enjoy solitude as much as anybody and probably more than most, but I'm neither a lottery winner nor the wastrel son of a billionaire industrialist (although I wish I were), so pulling a Thoreau isn't an option financially. The fact that I love my wife and dogs—and even the cat—too much to spend more than a few days apart from them, rules out the Gauguin maneuver; and I wouldn't have it any other way. Besides, if I just want to hide from the world, I can turn off the telephone, put on a set of headphones, and for all intent and purposes disappear into my house. Escaping can be a bonus, but it's not the main goal.

That goal may well be different every time I go out on a boat, wherever that boat brings me. The Highland Lakes of central Texas put me in the middle of the Texas Hill Country, the place that feels more like home to me than anywhere else in the world. The Gulf of Mexico, with its warm water and myriad ports from Mexico to Florida, offers the opportunity to see at least a little bit of the world as I cruise from place to place at my own pace. And the Puget Sound and Strait of Juan de Fuca

let me soak in spectacular scenery while surrounded by pods of orcas and Dahl's porpoises. Sometimes I go out to do nothing but float and think in quiet, other times I go to swim and live it up. Sometimes the fun is getting somewhere, sometimes the fun is having no particular place to go. Regardless of where I go or what I do while I'm there, some time on the water always puts things back in perspective and helps me remember that few things are really as critical to my life and well-being as I think they are.

HYDROTHERAPY

Here's an example. In the spring of 2001, I was going through a rather rough patch of life, one of those times when just opening your eyes each morning seems next to impossible and the least little thing can seem utterly catastrophic. The walls of my house were closing in on me like the jaws of a giant trash compactor. As I tried to battle through, I put my energies into my work, but found that wasn't the answer. Burdened as I was by outside stress, my work was suffering. And the more my work suffered, the more I suffered. It was a vicious cycle that had to be broken. So I put the dogs in the kennel and took my wife, Carey, up to Seattle, where we boarded a 28-foot Bayliner cuddy cabin. We cruised all around the San Juan Islands, watching orcas, before we finally docked for a few days at Sooke Harbour House in Sooke Harbour, Vancouver, one of the finest yet least-known getaways in North America. Then we took our sweet time heading back.

For that week, we were a million metaphorical miles from home and all its hassles. And each day those hassles seemed less and less devastating and more and more manageable, so that when we did go home we were both completely recharged and ready to deal with everyday life.

It's hard to make those Monday meetings in Dallas if you've taken the boat to Mexico.

The barometer of my recovery, during that entire trip, was my desire to get back to work. The first two or three days, all I wanted was solitude. Then I started checking my voice mail and returning a few calls. Next I started reading and answering my e-mails. By the time we set course for Seattle from Sooke Harbour, I was working more or less full time—and it didn't seem like drudgery anymore. I even started to look forward to getting back to my desk, which I'd begun thinking of as a torture device. All it took was a week on the water.

My troubles, obviously, didn't vanish during that trip, but my inability to deal with them did. So I started thinking about having a functional, onboard office in order to take advantage of the restorative powers of time on the water.

Luckily, my job didn't vanish during that trip either. As a writer, I have a great deal more career flexibility than most people, and getting away isn't particularly problematic. As long as I have cellular phone service and electricity for my laptop, I can work anywhere, including the cabin of a Bayliner. Carey's position with a nonprofit animal welfare group gives her a similar flexibility. Without question, we're lucky.

> "For some people, the boat is a floating apartment that never leaves the marina."

WORKING AND BOATING

But even if jobs don't have the kind of flexibility that lets you get out on the water whenever your fancy strikes, more and more employers are willing to allow their employees to work remotely. It takes serious discipline to seat yourself in front of a notebook computer and hammer out a report when you're adrift on a sparkling lake on a perfect summer day, but think about this: Wouldn't you rather work in the sunshine and fresh air with a view of the harbor or hills than in a conference room slogging through yet another meeting, or imprisoned in an office—even a corner office? Suddenly, buckling down and wrapping up that spreadsheet, dressed in nothing but a swimsuit and listening to your favorite music, doesn't seem like such a chore.

Even with a flexible job, though, you have to be ready for the possibility of getting by on a significantly reduced income if you're planning on spending an extended period living and working onboard. All the economic gripes you hear from those who've made the move to work from home—reduced opportunities for extra income by doing extra work, reduced opportunity for advancement—are compounded if you're not just working from home, but from a boat that usually has no fixed address. It's hard to make those Monday meetings in Dallas if you're docked in Mexico. So it's crucial, before taking the plunge, to examine your lifestyle and take a cold, hard look at your ability and desire to trade financial and career security for the pleasures of living and working onboard.

You also have to be realistic about your experience and ability as a boater. I've been on and around boats more or less my whole life. I've piloted everything from a standup personal watercraft to a 48-foot yacht. I've docked a twin-engine cruiser in windy conditions when one engine wasn't working, and I can read nautical charts nearly as well as I can read road maps. I tell you this not to brag, but to explain why I'm as comfortable at the helm of a boat, even in rough water, as I am behind the wheel of an SUV on a bone-dry highway.

Of course, it's entirely possible to live and work onboard your boat without even knowing how to start the engine. For some people, the boat

Instant safety test: Could you swim to shore from where you drop anchor?

on which they live and work is essentially a floating apartment that never leaves the marina slip. And if that's what you want, that's fine. I often want to spend a couple of days on a boat without ever starting the motor, just to be near the water and to put some space between myself and everyday life.

BE PREPARED

Whatever your plans, I highly recommend taking a few classes or reading a couple of seamanship books to brush up and improve your skills as a boater. While the title is a bit embarrassing, *The Complete Idiot's Guide to Boating and Sailing* will give you a good grasp of the basics, from engines to boat handling. A more dignified work is *Chapman Piloting: Seamanship & Boat Handling* (Chapman Piloting Seamanship and Boat Handling, 64th ed.) by Elbert S. Maloney and Charles Frederic Chapman. On the Internet, Boatsafe.com (*www.boatsafe.com*) not only

> ### TIP
> You can take a U.S. Coast Guard-approved boat safety course on-line at *www.boatsafe.com*

has a huge amount of information, but also offers on-line boating courses. Best of all, though, would be to take a U.S. Coast Guard Power Squadron course. Courses are offered nationwide. (Some states and localities require completion of a USCG or other boating course to receive a boat operator's license. Check your local rules and regulations and be sure to comply.)

MORE IS BETTER

The more you know about how your boat and the various systems onboard operate, the better. You might have to be your own mechanic if you have a problem offshore, and you have to be able to fix the little things that will go wrong even if you never leave the slip. Circuit breakers are going to cut off, belts and hoses will eventually fail, water lines are going to clog, and you're going to go broke in a hurry paying for a mechanic to come out to your boat every time a fuse needs replacing.

If you have even the foggiest notion of going out into open water, you must take a few seamanship classes to learn proper handling skills, especially if you've spent your whole life boating on more protected waters. If you don't know what you're doing when the water gets big, you may not be living or working on your boat much longer.

It's very important to remember that while everyone onboard doesn't have to be a Coast Guard-qualified captain, everyone must have basic boating skills. Even kids can learn to steer and operate the throttle well enough to pilot the boat toward safety if necessary. Having everyone learn the basics will not only improve your ability to handle a potential emergency, but it will give the captain much-needed relief from time to time.

SAFETY FIRST

I advise people, at least those foolhardy enough to engage me in conversation, to start small when it comes to spending time on a boat. Making the decision to spend a week, a month, or even a year onboard doesn't mean you also have to decide to spend that year circumnavigating the globe. I've spent more than ten years making my living on and around boats, and I've never made a day's trip of more than 100 miles. Nor have I ever gone more than 25 miles or so offshore. I've never made a run from Miami to St. Croix. The vast majority of my time is spent on the most prosaic bodies of water imaginable: bays, sounds, straits, and lakes. For years I had a rule that if I were spending the night onboard I wouldn't want to be any farther from shore than I could swim. I figured I could don a PFD [personal flotation device] and swim to safety if bad came to worse. As a result, I can say that I've never found myself in a situation that really even tested my abilities as a boater, and I'm proud of that. Anybody can get into trouble.

I've been lucky (knock wood), having never really had to worry about major health issues. Other people aren't so fortunate, but they still manage to spend days, weeks, months, and years onboard their boats by playing it smart, usually by choosing to make their home port close to their regular caregivers so that medical records and assistance are readily available. As with most everything in life, it's really just common sense. If you have a pertinent medical history—let's say you're diabetic—you shouldn't head off to Mexico for six months without at least a seven-months' supply of your medication on hand, along with a bilingual medical ID bracelet or dog tag so that if something goes wrong the local medics can make an informed diagnosis and treatment. This is especially important if you're going solo and won't have the luxury of an onboard support team (even a one-person team consisting of a friend or significant other) to come to your aid in an emergency.

Consider your family's needs before committing to a boat.

For reasons of safety, it's much smarter to live and work onboard with a partner, though there's a certain romance to spending time onboard solo. It's very Hemingway. You can sit around in your ratty trunks with no shirt, not brushing your teeth for days on end and living on little more than rum and Coke. You can enjoy the solitude, the "me against the elements" aspect (even if you never leave the dock), and the pleasure of watching your hair grow and your belly shrink. (One of the major benefits of spending a lot of time on a boat is that you lose weight. Partially because you become a bit more

Most people who live and work onboard are either childless or empty nesters, but that could change.

active, but mostly because it's a hassle to cook, especially if you're alone.) And there's no denying that it's a lot easier to move around onboard if you're the only passenger.

THE WHOLE CREW

I have enjoyed my single life on boats tremendously. But having had the insanely good luck of marrying someone who's been willing and able to drop everything and go boating with me pretty much whenever I want, wherever I want, and for as long as I want, I don't think I'd ever go solo again. Let's face it: There are very few things in life that aren't improved by sharing them with someone you love. And having been both single and half of a couple, I've found that having someone else onboard can be a great benefit. For one thing, if there are two of you onboard, you each only have to do half as much work. For another, someone else can call for help if the need arises. And as I'm going to say repeatedly, you'd

66 As long as you're physically and mentally capable, you can do this. 99

better prepare for that eventuality. The worst thing that can happen on a boat is the thing you don't prepare for.

Families are a different story. I don't have kids of my own, so my only experience of spending time on a boat with a family is from when I was a kid myself. Even through the rosy fog of memory, those weren't the best of times. I remember being cramped, bored, and cranky pretty much from the moment we got on the boat until a week or two after we were back home. Those were different times, though, back in the days before satellite TV and radio, before portable DVD players and video games. In those days, kids' onboard entertainment consisted of books (comic and other), board games, and beating up your little sister. Today, many more entertainment options make life onboard more palatable for kids. Some things, though, haven't and probably won't ever change, such as the fact that family members need privacy, not just from other boaters but from each other, and that means a larger, more expensive boat.

The most important family factor is your kids' attitude toward the enterprise. I know there are people who will argue that you shouldn't let

Spending a day onboard in nasty weather is a reality check.

your kids run your life, but if your kids don't want to be onboard, your life will be miserable. Don't ignore the signals. Some excellent advice I've heard is to pick a nearby marina as your home port and never go on more than a weekend trip if you have the whole family along. This way, the kids are still close to their friends and activities and you're never in the horrible position of facing a five-day cruise home, in close quarters, with a thirteen-year-old who hates you. Such a scenario may explain why most people who make the decision to live and work onboard are either childless or empty nesters.

In fact, if you make the move to a water-based lifestyle, you may be surprised to find that the majority of your cohorts are of retirement age or older. Think about it for a minute, though, and it starts to make perfect sense. As long as you're on a powerboat, boating's generally no more strenuous than you make it. (Sailing is a different beast entirely, requiring much more physical strength and ability.) If you stay at or very near the marina on a lake or protected bay, your boating may never get more arduous than driving a car. So there's no physical barrier to prevent you from living out your golden years onboard.

Add in the fact that older people are more likely to have a little money saved up and may be able to live on less income, since they've probably already bought every toy and goodie they might want or need. Also, once the kids are out on their own there's not so much reason to stay tied down to that big house. Why so many live-aboards are in their fifties, sixties, and beyond becomes obvious.

That could change, though, because more people in their twenties, thirties, and forties have careers that allow them to work remotely. (Not so long ago, even if the kids had moved out by the time you were in your early- to mid-fifties, your job most likely required your attendance at the office every day, making it almost impossible for you to live onboard until you retired.) And most of the other obstacles that might keep you from making a go of living and working on your boat are more perception than reality. As long as you're physically capable and mentally competent, you can do this if you really want to. You can do it solo, you can do it as a couple—you can even do it as a family if you work to accommodate everyone. All you really need is the desire.

Before you make the decision to live and work onboard for an extended period, however, you should first go out and spend a day on your boat in truly rotten conditions, when the rain's falling hard and cold, when the wind's blowing something fierce. Drop anchor. Turn off everything electric and ride it out. Don't be crazy and go out in a hurricane, but endure a seriously unpleasant day on the water a couple of times and see if your enthusiasm for the endeavor remains. If it doesn't, that's okay, because you can still go out and enjoy boating every chance you get, and you'll avoid making a mistake you'll regret. But if you're still fired up about living and working onboard after experiencing some rough conditions, you're ready to take the plunge.

CHAPTER 2

CHOOSING A BOAT

ONCE YOU'VE MADE THE DECISION TO SPEND SOME TIME, WHETHER IT'S A WEEK OR A YEAR, LIVING AND WORKING ON A BOAT, YOU HAVE TO CHOOSE THE RIGHT BOAT. THE ETERNAL BATTLE AMONGST BOATERS IS POWER V. SAIL (AKA SMOKE V. RAG), AND LIKE ALL AGE-OLD FEUDS (SEE: HATFIELDS V. MCCOYS), THERE'S NO SETTLING THIS.

I'm a powerboater and always have been. Make no mistake: I like sailing, especially the strange quiet that surrounds a sailboat on the move. But I must confess to being somewhat lazy. I would much rather turn a key and lean on a throttle to get where I'm going than perform the elaborate choreography that sailing requires. If you ever want an essentially good-for-nothing guest on your sailboat, I'm your guy. If, on the other hand, you want to kick back while I motor us from here to eternity, you're welcome to come along.

CONTENTS

► Size Matters

► Democracy Rules

► Powerboats

► Sailboats

► Houseboats and Trawlers

When making a purchase, consider the activities you plan to pursue once you're on the water. This Viking 61 is equipped for some serious fishing.

Sailboats and powerboats work equally well as offices. Stick with what you know.

As for a boat to work from, I don't think there's much difference between power and sail. With the right interior layout, either can work as home offices, so it's really just a matter of personal preference. If you grew up sailing around Martha's Vineyard, then by all means stick with the rags. And if you grew up like I did, skiing behind a smoker, stay with it. Go with what you know. No one really cares whether you're a sailor or a power boater. What's important is that boaters be considerate of each other.

When you start looking at the reality of working onboard, you'll soon realize that the power source—be it a V8 or 200 yards of sailcloth—has virtually no connection to your ability to work in comparison with the size and layout of the boat. The only time the power source matters is when you're under way, a time when you can't work on much anyway, since you're completely occupied with piloting your vessel.

SIZE MATTERS

The most important criterion for the boat you choose to live and work on is its size. Size matters. It matters more than everything else combined and multiplied by a million. Anybody who even hints otherwise is lying.

Yes, budget matters, but it should only be allowed to affect how new your boat is. It may be a harsh truth, but if you can't afford a boat big enough to live and work on comfortably, you can't afford to live and work on your boat.

One thing to bear in mind about boats, especially if you're not that familiar with boat design, is that the architectural limitations on size and layout are brutal. A boat's primary function is to travel in and on water, which means that the primary concern of the designer/architect/engineer team is to create a hull that will move well in and on water. There are plenty of outstanding books on the market that treat this subject with the depth and technical detail it requires, so I'll not get into it any more deeply than this. (Two particularly good books on the subject are *Understanding Boat Design*, by Ted Brewer, and *How to Design a Boat*, by John Teale.) Suffice it to say that the first and greatest restriction on a marine designer or architect is the requirement to design around a hull that performs well in the water. This is why there seem to be few variations in cabin and cockpit layout, even though there are vast numbers of boat makes and models on the market.

Another thing to remember is that size is somewhat relative. If you're 5'8", 140 pounds, and accustomed to living in a one-room, 200-square-foot apartment, you'll be much less cramped and claustrophobic living and working aboard a 28-foot boat than would be somebody my size—6'2", 225 pounds—who's used to living alone in a 3,000-square-foot house. And the only way to find out which boats have as much space as you need to feel comfortable is to look at a lot of them and see for yourself.

I can, however, help narrow things down by sharing my rules of thumb for how big a boat should be to live and work onboard comfortably. As noted, there are myriad different makes and models on the market, but rather than try and give each one even a quick mention, I'll take the Sea Ray fleet for my points of reference. From 26 feet to 70 feet, Sea Ray has a model in virtually every possible size. Detailed information on each of these boats is available online at Sea Ray's website: *www.searay.com*. [Websites for many other manufacturers can be found on page 173.]

> Size matters. It matters more than everything else combined and multiplied by a million.

Boats like the 31-foot Sundancer (above) can accommodate two people—if they're really close. The table can be pulled down to form a platform for cushions (inset).

GOING SOLO

▶ **260 Sundancer**

▶ **280 Sundancer**

▶ **300 Sundancer**

In case you're new to all this, the numbers in a boat's model designation generally refer to the boat's length overall (LOA), so a 260 is usually 26'0" in length. You can reasonably expect a 2650 to measure about 26'6" in length, and so on, unless the manufacturer ignores this custom entirely, as is the case here, and simply uses the designation to indicate that one boat is larger than another. It's terribly confusing, but the boat builders carry on in spite of my protest.

As big as I am, I can't imagine actually spending an extended period onboard a boat smaller than 28 feet. However, you might be able to live and work onboard something as small as 26 feet if you're going it alone. I think you'll regret it, but that's for you to find out. I like space. One thing's for sure, though: If you're not alone, you shouldn't even consider a boat with an LOA of less than 30 feet.

The boats mentioned above will accommodate one person fairly comfortably. The 28-foot 260 Sundancer is best-suited for long weekends or possibly week-long outings. A full month on one would be hard to handle. There's just not that much room onboard, and the bed is a V-berth that doubles as a couch and a dining area, impressive in terms of versatility but not so great when it comes to sleeping night after night. The V-berth is created by placing filler cushions on the dinette table, so it might not be the best thing for your back. Storage is also in desperately short supply on a 26-foot boat. But if you don't mind sleeping on the dinner table or owning only three changes of clothes, you can make it on such a boat.

I've spent some time on the 280 Sundancer, which actually has an LOA of 31'1", and it's a great setup for a solo. Even a couple could get by with this boat if they're really close. For long weekends, you can even fit a family. Worth bearing in mind is that even a boat this big and roomy has a dry weight of only 8,500 pounds, making it towable by many full-size and premium SUVs as well as heavy-duty pickups. The Chevy Suburban, for example, can easily accommodate the 280 Sundancer and trailer, giving you the option of living and working onboard your boat while enjoying waters across the country.

At 33'4", the 300 Sundancer is right on the border between a single's boat and one fit for couples. And at this point, you're getting into a size of boat whose dimensions I feel most comfortable in, even when alone. The 300 Sundancer can sleep six, but it starts to feel crowded at that point. I've found that boat manufacturers' brochures tend to overstate their boats' actual capacities by about double. If a boat claims to sleep four, figure two can sleep comfortably. If the boat is advertised to sleep six, like the 300 Sundancer, figure three comfortably, or maybe four if you don't mind snuggling.

Aside from being large enough for a single to live and work in comfortably, boats in the 28- to 33-foot range are seaworthy enough to make a Key West-Bimini run with no worries, or a trip from Galveston to New Orleans. This is important because, sooner or later, if you're spending a few months or even a year onboard, you're going to have to suffer through some rough weather and bad water. When you do, you'll

TIP

If you intend to tow a boat, check your auto insurance. Some policies cover the boat while in tow, and others do not.

want to be in a boat that can handle it. This isn't such a big deal if you stay on an inland lake and hardly ever leave the marina, but the vast majority of people I've known who've lived and worked onboard have gone for an extended cruise or two during their stay, and they're unanimous in their agreement that seaworthiness is a crucial trait. Although it can be harder to move around on land, a longer boat gives you more options in the water.

A 30-foot boat looks pretty big, but you'll notice straightaway that there's really not that much living space down below. By moving onto a boat this size, you'll basically be moving into a very small one-room apartment, where you cook, eat, sleep, and work in the same place. The only privacy onboard is in the head/shower, which, in many cases, is the vertical equivalent of a sensory-deprivation pod. That's why I say that boats this size are really for singles. Even the most loving couples occasionally need a little privacy, and it's just not there on a boat in this range unless one of you stays below, in the cabin, while the other hangs out above, in the cockpit.

Boats between 35 and 42 feet, like the 36-foot Beneteau below, have enough space and comfort for two, although the galley (inset) will still be compact.

The 360 Sundancer above, with an LOA of 39 feet, has a spacious salon suitable for entertaining (inset).

ROOM FOR TWO

▶ **320 Sundancer**

▶ **340 Sundancer**

▶ **360 Sundancer**

▶ **380 Sundancer**

▶ **390 Motor Yacht**

When you get to this range, approximately 35 to 42 feet, you reach a point where you're able to get some real space and comfort, enough for two people to spend a lot of time together without getting on each other's nerves. You're also starting to get into serious money if you're looking at new construction. However, you can find lots of "gently used" boats in this range for substantially less than you'd pay for a new one. (We'll get into that in a little more detail later.)

Boat handling skills become critical in this range. Once you pass 35 feet, you're definitely dealing with a twin-engine setup that will command a whole new respect for how much space the boat needs to do things like turn and stop, especially at higher speeds. If you're not experienced with boats of this size, it's imperative that you complete a hands-on seamanship course before delivery so that you're able to keep yourself and everyone else on the water safe. Most dealerships that carry boats this size and larger offer training. Take them up on it.

Onboard bathrooms, or heads, range from small and utilitarian (left) to elegant (right), depending on the size and make of the boat.

In addition to all that, you have to start thinking three-dimensionally with boats this big. Using the 320 Sundancer as an example, the draft with the drive down (the running position) is 43 inches. Meaning that to operate safely, you must be in water at least four feet deep, and you should use great caution anytime you find yourself in a depth of less than five feet. In deep-water areas, such as the Pacific Coast, where the land tends to drop sharply into the sea, this may not be much of an issue. But on inland waters and the Gulf of Mexico, where the bottom can slope so gradually that you walk 300 yards from the shore and stand in knee-deep shallows, this sort of draft means you have to know the area and be careful in planning your cruises so you don't run aground. Again, this is where that seamanship course will pay off, teaching you how to read charts and use depth sounders, as well as employing other safe operating techniques.

Another point to note is that when you get to this size range and larger, you're quickly losing the ability to tow your boat from place to place. While the 260 Sundancer has a dry weight of 6,200 pounds, well within the towing capabilities of even a midsize SUV such as the Ford Explorer, the 320 Sundancer weighs in at 13,800 pounds, requiring at least fifth-wheel capability from a tow vehicle. That limits your towing options to heavy-duty or commercial pickups. Realistically, once you pass the 10,000-pound dry weight point, you're going to be putting the boat in the water and leaving it there.

With an LOA of 35'6" and an 11'5" beam (maximum width), the 320 Sundancer is big enough for a couple to live and work onboard comfortably. I like the 200-gallon fuel tank, too. That may sound like a boatload of gas (pun intended), but unless you're going to be staying pretty close to shore in a coastal area or entirely on an inland lake, where you can pretty much count on being within five to seven miles of a marina with a gas dock, 200 gallons of fuel is about the bare minimum. I guarantee you don't want to find yourself 25 miles offshore and running on fumes.

The 340 Sundancer is a significant increase in size and power, 37'6" in length and sporting a 12-foot beam, with a pair of 6.2L V8 engines providing muscle. The engines are important in boats this size, because they have to overcome both the boat's dry weight (14,000 lbs for the 340 Sundancer) and the drag resulting from the size of the hull, something that plays a substantial role at all speeds. While a 22-foot runabout with a top speed of 55 miles per hour may, at speed, only have a few square feet of hull in contact with the water, a boat this size has a square meter or more touching the water, even at full throttle. This added hull contact means added drag, which means you need bigger, stronger engines to drive you. At the same time, bigger, stronger engines drink more gas, so even if the fuel capacity is increased compared to smaller boats (the 340 Sundancer holds 225 gallons of gas, 25 gallons more than the 320 Sundancer), the cruising range may not be much greater, if at all.

A similar thing happens when you step up from the 340 Sundancer to the 360 Sundancer. You get a bigger boat (39'0" LOA, 12'6" beam, 18,500-lb dry weight), bigger engines (a pair of 8.1L V8s), but not that much more fuel capacity (250 gallons). However, with the step-up to the 360 Sundancer, you move up to what Sea Ray calls the Sport Yacht classification. This means that you're now in the category where living and working onboard is more like living and working in a small studio apartment instead of a one-room flat. At this size, boats are able to offer amenities such as a full galley and a private stateroom (bedroom) that can be closed off so you can have some measure of privacy even if you're

> **" Two hundred gallons of fuel is a bare minimum. "**

not the only person below decks.

The next step up, the 380 Sundancer, is a 42-footer big enough for even a small family. The forward stateroom gives privacy and can be the master bedroom for Mom and Dad while a kid or even two (as long as they're small enough to share a semiconfined space peacefully) can sleep in the midcabin/galley area.

The 390 Motor Yacht and its ilk are the entry-level versions of the boat you probably envision when you think of living and working onboard in style. The enclosed cockpit that rises above the cabin, the swooping lines, and the large cabin windows combine to embody the concept of "yacht" for most of us. With an LOA of 41'9", this is a hair shorter than the 380 Sundancer, but its 14'3" beam makes it feel much, much roomier. The elevated cockpit design, of which I'm a huge fan, also allows the 390 Motor Yacht to offer staterooms forward and aft, so you can have a bedroom and an office onboard, or you can give the kids their own quarters.

Not that you need kids to enjoy the space. A New Yorker named Kent Doyle, for example, lives alone onboard his 40-plus-foot trawler *Manatee*, and uses the second stateroom for guests. He can work on his laptop and when the spirit moves him, invite friends for a cruise to Nantucket or Block Island. He calls the *Manatee* his "moveable feast."

FAMILY STYLE

▶ **400 Sedan Bridge**

▶ **420 Sundancer**

▶ **450 Express Bridge**

▶ **480 Motor Yacht**

Moving the whole family onboard for an extended period isn't everybody's cup of tea, although some families do it every year. Tom and Nan MacNaughton, who have lived and worked on boats for fifteen years and raised a daughter onboard, are firm believers that a boat is the very best place for a family. On their website (*www.macnaughtongroup.com*), they write: "If you take your children to live on a boat you are probably taking them to a less polluted, safer environment. They can be with the people they love the most all the

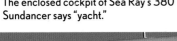

The enclosed cockpit of Sea Ray's 380 Sundancer says "yacht."

time. They will travel. They will meet and become comfortable with and able to deal with people of all ages and from different cultures and subcultures. They will become far more self-reliant and self-motivated than the average child. They generally turn out to be hardworking, goal-oriented people who at the same time are more relaxed and confident about life than the average."

This arrangement works best if you have very young kids who are still at peace with the idea of limited privacy and freedom. But for those who are not so young, there remains the problem of schooling, something all concerned parents must deal with. Of course, "home-schooling" might very well be the solution, provided the parents are willing to take on additional onboard duties.

If you have a family, boats like the ones listed above can accommodate more than just two people comfortably. As with every step

The 420 Sundancer's design gives three levels of living space and has two full staterooms. It's perfect for family fun and privacy.

up the food chain, this class of boats is significantly more expensive than the smaller ones. However, you're paying for space, a commodity that's all but priceless if you're going to be spending six months onboard with the entire family.

The Bridge design, such as the 400 Sedan Bridge, is ideal for a family because it not only provides separate staterooms, but it includes separate levels for parents and kids. Those separate spaces are a bonus when you're on a tight deadline: You can sequester yourself in the lower cabin and work while the others are two flights up on the bridge.

If three levels of separation aren't a requisite for your sanity and peace of mind, but you still want and need room for the family onboard, something like the 420 Sundancer may be more up your alley. It has more of a runabout look and feel. Even at 45 feet, boats like the 420 Sundancer are less intimidating for boaters who've spent their lives on ski boats and runabouts than the showier Bridge and Motor Yacht styles. Still, this model only gives you a stateroom and a salon (essentially a one-bedroom apartment layout), which may not be enough.

I love the 450 Express Bridge and every other boat that shares its design. For living and working, this is just about heaven. You get the bridge way up top, an upper cabin/cockpit that can sleep a couple of kids or overnight guests and offers a great open-air lounge area with access to the swim platform, plus the lower cabin. Two full staterooms and two full heads make this a floating two-bedroom/two-bath apartment—and only slightly less expensive than a two-bedroom/two-bath apartment in midtown Manhattan or San Francisco's Nob Hill. The property taxes are vastly more affordable, however, and your commute is the stuff of dreams.

About the biggest-small family boat falls in line with the 480 Motor Yacht, with an LOA of 50'5" and a 15'3" beam. If you're more of a traditionalist when it comes to boat design, it's quite possible that you'll prefer the Motor Yacht to the Bridge because it's a two-level design that, well, looks like the sort of boat you'd expect somebody to live and work on, while the Bridge design looks a bit racier and carefree.

Panoramic views of the Manhattan skyline are a bonus for New York City area boaters, and cheaper onboard than on land.

LIVING LARGE

- ▶ **510 Sundancer**
- ▶ **540 Cockpit Motor Yacht**
- ▶ **550 Sundancer**
- ▶ **560 Sedan Bridge**
- ▶ **600 Sun Sport**
- ▶ **680 Sun Sport**

The largest yachts, above 50 feet, may require a professional captain, but if you have the budget you can live in the lap of luxury onboard.

When you start looking at boats in the 50-foot-plus range, you're taking the concept of living and working onboard to a whole new level, a level we all aspire to but few of us actually reach. In this range, you're no longer worrying about having enough room for everyone onboard, or even about having enough privacy. Unless you're a very experienced and capable boater, you will, however, probably start worrying about hiring a captain if you're actually going to be heading out for a cruise. Even then you'll probably hire a captain for any extended point-to-point cruises so you can spend your time relaxing and/or working rather than manning the helm.

Houseboats are comfortable, but beware the so-called "death zone" on older models.

OTHER STYLES

Houseboats and pontoons are two styles that people frequently suggest when considering spending extended time onboard. It's just personal choice, but I find even the biggest pontoon too small to live and work onboard comfortably by myself, let alone with my wife and the menagerie. And even though they're great for idly tooling around a local lake or river, there's no way I'd ever take a pontoon out of sight of shore for even a minute. That rules out any possibility of living and working on the coast, even the Gulf Coast.

Houseboats have great space and may be brilliant choices on an inland body of water, even a big one, but older houseboats have some safety issues that make me very skittish about them. They tend to collect carbon monoxide in the space below the swim platform, leading to what's called—tragically—the "death zone." (*The Arizona Republic* published an excellent special report on this phenomenon that can be read on-line at: *www.azcentral.com/specials/houseboats/*). This makes houseboats, especially older models, risky for living and working onboard, even more so if you have kids who may swim.

The death zone is the area directly below the rear swim platform. The platform sits a foot or so above the water, creating a neat little hideout space where kids particularly enjoy congregating. If the houseboat's electric generator is running, however, the exhaust is directed to the rear of the boat and carbon monoxide collects in this space, creating a lethal hazard. "It is the scariest investigation I have ever done," Jane McCammon, a carbon monoxide expert with the National Institute for Occupational Safety and Health, told the Arizona Republic. "The carbon monoxide concentrations are so high where you have your children playing." The paper also reported that carbon monoxide concentrations were measured at 30,000 parts per million (ppm) in the death zone, twenty-five times the level of exposure (1,200 ppm) that's considered "immediately dangerous," according to McCammon, adding that even people sitting on the swim deck or slide were taking in carbon monoxide levels of 7,000 ppm.

Newer models have corrected the problem, but I have a more fundamental problem with houseboats: I'm a boater who wants a boat that looks like a boat, not like a floating trailer or cottage. Nevertheless, lots of people like the idea of having a marine atmosphere without sacrificing creature comforts, and houseboats may be ideal for them.

HOUSEBOATS

Houseboats or barges are especially popular with people who want to live onboard for a long time, because they're more spacious and more fully equipped than other types of boats. One reason for this is that their cruising range is limited at best. They're designed for use only in the most protected waters. In fact, some "floating homes," like those in the famous Sausalito, California houseboat community, are hardly boats at all. They have no self-propulsion. But these townhouses-on-rafts do tend to allow for the space their owners desire, while also offering a life on the water. Some of them are downright sumptuous. And because these boats don't go anywhere, their owners need to worry much less about securing their possessions against water and turbulence than do those whose homes are made for cruising. Floating-home marinas are often thriving communities in their own right, as the more stable lifestyle encourages the residents to get to know one another.

"It's like a little village," one Sausalito houseboat owner described her community to the *San Francisco Chronicle*. Other Sausalito residents are equally enthusiastic and say they plan to stay there for life.

TRAWLERS AND TUGS

Other liveaboards, like Kent Doyle, choose trawlers or tugs as "happy mediums." The bigger, boxier shape of this type of boat allows more headroom, more space, and more of a houselike ambiance than traditional sailboats and powerboats. But unlike houseboats, trawlers are also seaworthy. Among trawler and tug enthusiasts are many former sailors. In fact, Jerry Husted, founder of Nordic Tug in Bainbridge Island,

TIP

Look for used boats on-line and through classified ads in boating publications such as *Soundings*.

Above: New Yorker Kent Doyle lives aboard a classic 44-foot trawler with two bedrooms and two baths. Boats over 40 feet, like his, offer real space and privacy.

Bottom: A trawler's interior is spacious because of its boxy design. Note the exterior door on the Nordic Tug below—almost full height, very like those leading to a patio at home.

Even though trawlers are built for comfort, not speed, they can still travel at a brisk pace.

Washington, reports that half the buyers of his boats are former sailors. Ann Pettengill, a longtime sailor who owns an Island Packet moored in Wickford, Rhode Island, explains: "Sailors love the feel of the water and of the wind. They love being close to the water. Because sailboats only go about eight or nine knots, you really get a feel of the water. Powerboats go zipping through the water and don't have that sense of closeness to the elements that you get from a sailboat. Trawlers are comfortable— they give all the creature comforts of a 'house on water,' but they don't go that fast. Many sailors choose a trawler because it only goes about ten knots. You're still on the water—you can get from A to B just like you did when you were sailing—but it's much easier on the body. Trawlers are almost like mini-houseboats in that respect."

Going on-line is an efficient way to shop for new and used boats. A 2003 Hunter 426 like the one above was recently offered on-line at $225,000. A 2002 Hunter 426 was advertised at $184,000.

NEW OR USED?

Once you've chosen the type of boat you want, you have another decision to make: new or used? Power boaters and sailors may have a blood feud going, but it's nothing compared to the fierceness of disagreement between people who fervently believe you should always buy a new boat and those who swear you're dumber than a box of rocks if you don't buy used. As is so often the case, both sides have points worth hearing, but neither has an exclusive on the truth.

I've always been a fan of buying new whenever possible, whether we're talking about boats, cars, or anything else that requires taking out a long-term loan from the bank. I like being the first and only owner of something. I like getting the full warranty. I like having the newest, shiniest, best gear possible.

I completely understand, though, the philosophy that says if you buy a used boat you'll save an enormous amount of money, giving yourself the option of either keeping more of your life's savings to spend on other stuff or buying a much larger, better-equipped boat for the price you'd have paid for a new but smaller one.

Those are both valid arguments, and now I'm going to let you in on a secret. Generally speaking, there are very few things that can go seriously wrong on a boat. Sure, the engines can fail, but they can also be replaced. So can the electronic components and the wiring if necessary, although that's a bit of a hassle. As far as the structural integrity of a boat goes, there's not much to worry about. Wooden structural components may develop rot, but even that's not nearly the concern it was a few years ago. Fiberglass can delaminate. That's about it. And if there's a problem with either of these, it'll show up pretty quickly because it's the result of defective materials, not long-term wear and tear. This means that if you find a fifteen-year-old boat that's structurally sound, the odds are very strong that it will remain structurally sound as long as you own it, provided you give it proper maintenance.

You can save a huge amount of money buying a used boat, although you have to be sure you're making accurate comparisons when you're shopping. Here's an example:

I went on-line to MarineMax.com (*www.marinemax.com*) and researched the price of a 2003 Sea Ray 340 Sundancer (new at the time). MarineMax posted the MSRP as $256,547, with an option package driving the price up. Then I went to Boats.com (*www.boats.com*) and found a 2000 Sea Ray 340 Sundancer, with all the bells and whistles, for $120,000. So I could have saved myself at least $136,547 by going with the used boat. To be honest, I probably would've been extremely happy with it.

Then I did more in-depth research. The 2003 340 Sundancer, according to Sea Ray, has an LOA of 37'6" and a 12'0" beam. But the 2000 model listed on Boats.com showed an LOA of 35' and a beam of 11'5". That may not sound like a lot, just 2'6" shorter and 7" narrower, but on a boat every inch matters. So now I was able to make an informed decision. I could give up a little space and save a ton of money or I could pay about double what the 2000 model would cost to get a bigger, newer boat.

TIP

New or used, it is your responsibility, not the manufacturer's or owner's, to make sure your boat is in compliance with state and federal regulations.

BIG SAVINGS, BUT PROBLEMS, TOO

One problem with buying used boats is that they're not like used cars, filling the back lot of every dealership in town. To find a used boat, you'll probably have to either go on-line or prowling through the newspapers and trader magazines, and then you may very well have to do some traveling. The used 340 Sundancer I found was in Miami. I was in Austin, about 1,700 miles away, so I couldn't just bop over and have a walkaround or even take it out for a quick demo spin. I'd have to be pretty set on buying the thing just to justify the time and expense of getting myself to Miami. I may have been able to find a comparably equipped and priced boat a bit closer to home, but most likely I still would've had to do at least a bit of traveling.

Traveling to try out a used boat isn't the only expense, either. If you buy a boat even a few hundred miles away, you'll have to deal with the hassles and expense of having it delivered, unless it's small enough to tow with your own vehicle. And unless you buy through a dealer, there may well be other issues you'll have to deal with, like not having a warranty. (Even if you buy used from a dealer, you may have to pay extra to get a warranty.)

You'll pay a lot more for a new boat, but you'll also get some added benefits, like the convenience of working with a local dealer. I can go over to Boat Town in Austin, where my friend Clayton Raven can show me a nice selection of boats to take out for a demo ride. (I can go to Sail & Ski, South Austin Marine, or any of the other dealers in the area and have a similar experience.) When I've made my decision, Clayton will arrange to have the boat delivered to the waterway of my choice. There, a Boat Town representative will spend the day on the water with me and make sure I understand how to operate everything on the boat, from starting the motor and easing away from the dock to putting up the canvas.

You also have the security of knowing that the dealership can and will handle any sort of mechanical work that may need to be done, and that they'll process the warranty claims. All this adds up to a large measure of peace of mind that's hard to put a price tag on.

GASOLINE OR DIESEL?

A final consideration is choosing between gasoline and diesel engines. Like so many aspects of living and working onboard, there's no right or wrong answer. Generally speaking, diesel power will give you better fuel economy, while gasoline is more readily available— especially on inland waters—but these aren't hard and fast rules. The boat builders don't make the decision any easier for us, as most of them offer virtually every model with either diesel or gas power.

My guidelines for choosing diesel or gas are pretty simple: Research the waters you'll be spending time on and make your power choice

> "Whether you choose diesel or gasoline will depend on where your boat is going."

accordingly. If you're going to be living and working, for instance, on Lake Lanier, outside Atlanta, for instance, and you discover that there are only a couple of fuel docks that offer diesel, then common sense says to get a boat with gasoline engines. If you'll be in Seattle, where diesel is readily available, and you'll be making some long trips offshore—down to Portland, say, or San Francisco—you might want to pass on gasoline in order to take advantage of diesel's better fuel economy.

Choosing a boat isn't easy, even if you're only going to be onboard sporadically. It's a purchase on the order of buying a house, so you want to get it right. And aside from size considerations and the choice of fuel, you have to look at the intangibles and your personal desires.

GOING MOBILE?

Since I'm susceptible to wanderlust, I wanted to be able to split time between my "home" port of Lake Travis and the Gulf of Mexico, so purchasing a towable boat was appealing. But that would require keeping the boat's dry weight below 13,800 pounds, the absolute maximum towing capacity on the Ford F-350 King Ranch Super Duty pickup that I was eyeing as a potential tow vehicle.

At the same time, I had to be realistic about our spatial needs. We needed room for me, Carey, our three dogs—Mali, Curtis Ray and BabyLucy—and our cat, Tutu. Since Mali and Curtis Ray weigh about 90 pounds each (at 35 pounds, BabyLucy's the runt of the pack), they take up a pretty good chunk of real estate even when they're sleeping.

So I had a dilemma. I could opt for a super-sized boat, a 48-footer or larger, that would give us loads of room onboard but would essentially eliminate the possibility of going from Lake Travis to the Gulf, much less from Lake Travis to Puget Sound, without hiring a transporter. Or I could buy a towable boat and sacrifice onboard space.

DEMOCRACY RULES

I'd only gotten this far into the decision-making process when I had a moment of clarity and remembered that I wasn't the only one whose life would be affected by this choice. The dogs and cat I could safely impose my will upon, but Carey deserved an equal voice in the choice of

TIP

Log on to *www.nadaguides.com* for Blue Book Values.

"If you're going to be living onboard with anybody else, make sure you both have a say in everything there is to have a say about."

Above: The salon of a Cobalt 360. Below: the Sea Ray 340 Sundancer's stateroom. The boats have similar retail prices, but one's Blue Book value is higher, making it a better resale item.

both boat and home port. If you're going to be spending any time at all on a boat, in a confined space, with anyone else, you'd better make sure that you both have a say in everything there is to have a say about.

The first joint decision was to choose the right boat for us. After that, we could worry about where we'd keep it. Carey agreed that it would be good to have a boat we could tow from place to place if the urge proved too strong to resist. She also agreed that if push came to shove, we'd give up trailerability for spatial comfort. Since there would be just the two of us onboard and the animals wouldn't need their own rooms, we didn't necessarily need a dedicated bedroom. We didn't, however, want to sleep on the dining room table.

Aesthetics were a consideration too. We both wanted something with elegant lines and a European flair. We agreed that no matter where we set up home port, we'd not be making many long-range offshore runs because of the animals, none of which are particularly good with heavy seas. That meant gasoline power would be our best choice.

We agreed that we'd buy new rather than used. This would stretch our budget to the absolute limit, but we were able to justify it. We had decided to live onboard full time: we knew some people who would live out of their boats on weekends, or for chunks of the warmer months, but we had a bigger dream. We wanted to try living onboard full-time for as much as an entire year. We would sell our house before purchasing the boat, essentially trading one mortgage for another. We'd be adding the expense of a marina slip, but we'd be eliminating property taxes, which, at about $500 a month, cost about the same. When the time came for us to be landlubbers again, we'd sell the boat and buy another house, most likely less expensive than our current home, to offset the loss we knew we'd take on the resale of the boat.

Still, we didn't want to lose any more money than necessary, so we wanted a boat that would hold as much resale value as possible. Considering depreciation, we might have been better off buying a used boat, since we were essentially planning to sell it off after a year anyway. But we didn't want to hassle with shopping for and dealing with a used boat. (A year may seem like a long time, but it's really not, and neither Carey nor I wanted to spend any of it dealing with annoying problems.)

A new boat would give us as much trouble-free time onboard as possible, we felt, as long as we chose one of the highest possible quality.

We narrowed our search to a pair of boats, Cobalt's 360 and Sea Ray's 340 Sundancer. Both had similar retail prices, in the $250,000 range (the Cobalt's base MSRP with twin MX6.2 MPI Mercruiser engines was $257,480, the base 340 Sundancer with identical engines was $256,547). The lines were similar, although Carey and I both slightly favored the Cobalt's styling. We liked the 340 Sundancer's interior a little better, though, and the 340 Sundancer had the edge in overall size, with an LOA of 37'6", a full 18" longer than the Cobalt 360's 36'0" LOA, and a 12'0" beam, 18" wider than the Cobalt's 10'6". It was about as close a call as you could imagine.

Then we did some resale research and the 360 became the unquestioned winner. Looking at the National Automobile Dealer's Association (NADA) Blue Book values (see on-line listings at *www.nadaguides.com*), we found that a base year-old 340 Sundancer had an average resale value of $162,050, while a base year-old Cobalt 360 had an average resale price of $196,360, over $30,000 more than the Sea Ray. A two-year-old Cobalt 360 had an average resale value of $177,100, higher than a one year newer comparable Sea Ray. The evidence was undeniable. The Cobalt would return more money on resale than the Sea Ray, no matter how quickly we resold it. Carey and I revisited both boats and agreed that while the Cobalt would be a tighter fit physically, the financial benefits far outweighed that consideration.

All this could have been avoided, of course, if we had already owned a seaworthy, suitably spacious boat. There's absolutely no reason you can't move onboard the trusty cruiser you've owned for twenty years as long as it has sufficient room. Although there have been tremendous technological advances in the world over the past fifty years, boats have remained blissfully similar. A 45-footer from 1955 may not have as many built-in amenities as a 45-footer from 2003, but thanks to those technological advances, you can buy literally everything you need to retrofit that old '55 and make it a superb craft to live and work onboard here and now.

SPACE AND POWER

The only real obstacles to transforming the boat you already own into the boat you live and work on are space and power. No matter what you do, you can't make a 24-foot cuddy cabin work. Nor can you make a 28-foot deck boat or a 32-foot center console fishing boat a suitable candidate for long-term living and working onboard. You have to have shelter and a place to sleep. You also have to have shore power, the ability to plug your boat's electrical system into the electricity from the dock, but this feature can be added as a retrofit to just about any boat.

An onboard electric generator will provide power, but I recommend using shore power whenever possible. It's safer, since it doesn't use gas or have an exhaust. The onboard generator is great if you're going to overnight at anchor, but if shore power is available, use it.

I hadn't really considered the possibility of renting a boat for this adventure, mostly because I'd not heard of anyone from whom I could rent a boat of this size for a whole year or even six months. Especially when they found out I'd be bringing three big dogs and a cat. Even if such a place existed, I figured the price would be prohibitive. (Houseboats, for example, generally charter for about $2,000 to $2,500 per week.)

However, for people who just want to get out a few times a year for a week or two and have a working holiday, there's a recent development that's gaining popularity. Called fractional ownership, it's similar to the time-share concept. You join a syndicate and pitch in a portion of the purchase price, housing, and basic maintenance costs of a boat (called a share), and then you're allotted a comparable amount of time onboard. After a set period of time, the boat is resold and any profits dispersed according to number of shares owned. Fractional ownership has its positives and negatives, but if you want a boat for relatively short periods throughout the year, this arrangement may be perfect for you.

A company called Port & Starboard Boats (*www.psboats.com*) with offices in Austin, Texas, and Naples, Florida, offers fractional ownership of ski boats as well as cruisers suitable for living and working onboard. The Port & Starboard setup is a little different, in that there are no limits

to the number of shares sold and there's no upfront cost. You pay the monthly fees and your access to the boat is limited only by the first-come, first-served schedule shared with the other users. That schedule fills up pretty quickly for the summer months, of course, but the cost is affordable.

Fractional Yachts Inc. (*www.fractionalyachtsinc.com*), in Vancouver, B.C., is a more classic fractional ownership setup. In one case, you actually pay for a quarter of the boat, plus a monthly maintenance fee, and you get eighty-four days onboard per year—determined, of course, by the schedules of the other three owners. I like this setup best when it comes to part-time ownership because you know exactly what you're getting. If you don't mind spending the winter in Vancouver (it's near enough to the Pacific Ocean to make the climate pretty temperate year-round) you can all but assure yourself of an uninterrupted month or two onboard and still be in line for a week or two (or more) onboard during the summer.

Carey and I weren't planning to be part-timers, though. We were going to try and make a full year's go of it, and we didn't want artificial limits placed on us. We wanted to be able to take our boat anywhere we wanted, anytime we wanted—as long as we could arrange and afford transportation. So fractional ownership, leasing, renting, or chartering was out of the question for us. We were going to be full-on boaters and owners, living and working on our brand-new, fully loaded, 2003 Cobalt 360.

> We were going to be full-on owners, living and working on our new 2003 Cobalt 360, fully loaded.

CHAPTER 3

CHOOSING A HOME PORT

NOW THAT WE HAD A BOAT, WE HAD TO MAKE THE NEXT BIG DECISION: WHERE WOULD WE KEEP IT? CAREY AND I HAD EACH LIVED IN AUSTIN AT LEAST TWENTY YEARS, AND IT WAS HARD TO IMAGINE PICKING UP AND MOVING. AT THE SAME TIME, WE'D SPENT EXTENSIVE TIME IN ROCKPORT, TEXAS, ON THE GULF OF MEXICO, AND LOVED IT THERE. AND WE'D SPENT A SURPRISING AMOUNT OF TIME IN THE PACIFIC NORTHWEST AND HAD OFTEN DISCUSSED, ABSTRACTLY, THE POSSIBILITY OF MOVING THERE SOMEDAY. THIS, IT SEEMED, MIGHT BE THE PERFECT OPPORTUNITY.

Most people who choose to live and work onboard, I've found, fall into one of two camps: urbanites who are looking to cut their living and commuting hassles and expenses, and exiles who are looking to simplify their lives by going partially off the grid. Go to any major city in the United States—New York,

CONTENTS

▶ City or Solitude?

▶ Personal Needs

▶ One Couple's Choice

Where to drop anchor? Consider the life you want to lead and the facilities you'll want available.

Urban convenience (top), vacation-style escape (above).

Chicago, Los Angeles, San Francisco, Seattle—and you'll find all kinds of people who've given up on trying to find an affordable apartment within a reasonable drive of the city and so have moved onboard. These adventurers are simply tired of the usual grind and are making their own way.

Kent Doyle is a prime example of the urbanite who's opted out and moved onboard. In a short span, as he tells it, he saw both his multimillion-dollar software business and his marriage collapse. So he moved onboard the *Manatee*, which he'd bought fifteen years earlier, and began living at a marina slip just an eight-minute ferry ride from Manhattan's World Financial Center, where he catches a subway to his consulting clients. Tom and Nan MacNaughton, on the other hand, are adventurers. Tom is a yacht designer, and Nan is a freelance writer. With their family, they've spent years cruising the seas. Both types are extremely happy and successful by any measure, so it's not a question of which is the better lifestyle. The question is, which is *your* lifestyle?

Choosing a home port is often, if not always, a matter of your personal inclinations. If you're the type who wants the best of both worlds—living in an "apartment" within a $30 cab ride of nightclubs and restaurants—you'll gravitate toward the urban marina for a fraction of a luxury apartment's rental cost. Solitude seekers will be more likely to pick a small-town marina where privacy's a given and you can go for days without anybody even walking along your dock.

POINTS TO CONSIDER

Choosing a home port is a bit less complicated than choosing your boat, but there are questions you must ask yourself. For example:

▶ **How will you get your mail?**
▶ **Does the United States Postal Service deliver to the marina?**
▶ **Does FedEx or UPS deliver to the marina?**
▶ **How's the cellular telephone service?**
▶ **Can you get a landline telephone connection at the marina?**
▶ **What are the rules concerning liveaboards?**
▶ **Does the marina allow satellite dishes?**

You'd better find all this out before you sign a contract and then try to set up a remote office where there are no landlines, no mail service, spotty cellular service, and where satellite dishes aren't allowed. Ever try to run a business without telephones, faxes, Internet connection, or mail?

Carey and I discussed all this at length. We realized that we had a fairly demanding set of criteria for our home port.

▶ **We had to have a marina that would allow liveaboards in the first place. (A surprising number don't allow liveaboards at all, and many that do only allow them for a limited period, usually six months.)**
▶ **The marina had to have a restaurant and bar so we could occasionally get off the boat for a quick bite or a happy-hour beer.**
▶ **The marina had to allow long-term parking of our vehicle.**
▶ **The marina had to allow satellite dishes for our television and Internet connection.**
▶ **The marina had to allow pets. (You'd be surprised how many don't.)**

Sailing home to a port in Holland, Michigan, near the lighthouse known as Big Red.

▶ The marina had to have either landline telephone connectivity or, preferably, a location where we could receive a strong cellular signal.

▶ The marina had to be reasonably priced.

▶ The marina had to be within a short distance of a post office box, which we could use for snail mail.

Essentially, we wanted the same situation my friend Kent Bridges had at Pete's Harbor in Redwood City, California, on the southern tip of San Francisco Bay. Kent's a high-tech guy who rode the dot-com wave all the way to the crest and now specializes in start-ups. He also has a ranch in Utah where he and his wife, Deb, raise Arabian stallions. Deb lives full-time on the ranch in Utah, and Kent spends Mondays through Fridays on his old Chris-Craft 38 at Pete's Harbor. He doesn't have to pay the exorbitant rents of Silicon Valley. He gets to take his meals and enjoy a glass or two of wine at the Waterfront Restaurant at the marina. He can get to the San Jose airport and jet off to anywhere in the world in about an hour, boat to boarding gate.

Carey found the idea of moving from house to boat a radical enough change; neither of us really wanted to stray too far from familiar surroundings. There was only a certain amount of "unmooring" we felt we could handle. This is why you have to talk about these things. We ruled out the Pacific Northwest instantly, which we felt was too far from our security blankets. So it was a choice between Lake Travis and Rockport. Both offered everything we wanted. Rockport was a bit more affordable and had the allure of the Gulf, with potential trips to Galveston, Houston, New Orleans, and even Mexico. Lake Travis offered quick and easy access to Austin and the least amount of disruption to our lives.

In the end, the choice was made for us. I was offered a position as the on-air automotive critic for Austin's KTBC-TV and my "Street Beat" features would also air on Detroit's WJBK-TV. This was a tremendous professional break that anchored us in Lake Travis, where I'd be able to dash into Austin easily to film my automotive segments. It worked out

> "We decided we would sample various marinas, spending a few nights here and a few nights there to get an idea of them before committing."

This marina in Old Saybrook, CT, has picnic grounds, a swimming pool, and a restaurant on the premises, as well as easy access to business services.

well for Carey, too. With a base in Lake Travis, she would be able to keep a closer hand and eye on Catahoula Rescue, her non-profit animal rescue organization. As an added bonus, we'd be able to deal with Clayton Raven and Boat Town rather than a Cobalt dealership in Seattle or Rockport.

Another unexpected bonus came from our decision to settle in Lake Travis. Although the lake is 63 miles long, it's small enough to easily get anywhere on it in a single day, even if you have to go all the way from one end to the other. So instead of choosing a home port straightaway and making a yearlong commitment to a particular marina (there's enough demand for wet slips on Lake Travis that most marinas, especially those nearer Austin, are able to demand a year's lease as a minimum), we decided we would "sample" the various marinas, spending a few nights here and a few nights there to get an idea of each before committing. We got a P.O. box at a U.S. Post Office in a town just a few miles from a number of marinas, secure in the knowledge that we'd be able to check the mail as often as necessary, even if we fell in love with a marina at the other end of the lake.

Check electrical hookups at prospective marinas.

CHAPTER 4

SETTING UP THE OFFICE

WITH A BOAT LINED UP AND A PLAN FOR CHOOSING A HOME PORT IN MIND, IT WAS TIME TO GET DOWN TO THE NITTY-GRITTY: SETTING UP AN ONBOARD OFFICE THAT WOULD FUNCTION AS WELL AS THE OFFICE IN OUR HOUSE. IT WOULD HAVE TO BE HIGHLY COMPACT, HIGHLY MOBILE, AND VIRTUALLY IMPERVIOUS TO WATER AND ROUGH CONDITIONS. NO SMALL CHALLENGE.

Since I'd been working at home full-time for close to ten years, I thought setting up the onboard office would be a breeze. I already had most of the equipment I would need, and I was familiar with working remotely.

Then I decided I'd use this as an opportunity to upgrade all my gear. After all, I reasoned, I couldn't be expected to go onboard with outdated equipment when the newer versions were tougher, faster, smaller, and more

CONTENTS

▶ Computers
▶ Waterproofing
▶ Communications
▶ Installation

A successful onboard work space requires a minimalist approach, which means doing everything with the least possible amount of hardware and clutter.

> Space and electricity are in limited supply onboard. Equipment had better be able to pull double duty.

mobile. No more big, clunky printer. No more oversized desktop computer, even if I did love that generous, readable screen.

The first order of business was to make a list of exactly what we needed. I've seen enough cubicles to know that the basic office setup is pretty much the same for everyone. The only real difference is how much room you have. On a boat, you have very little.

We initially thought that we each needed the following:

- ▶ **A computer**
- ▶ **A modem**
- ▶ **A telephone**
- ▶ **An Internet connection**
- ▶ **A fax machine**
- ▶ **A copier**
- ▶ **A printer**

We'd also each need the usual supplies:

- ▶ **Reams of paper**
- ▶ **A few boxes of pens**
- ▶ **A dozen or so spiral notebooks**
- ▶ **A stapler**
- ▶ **A tape dispenser**
- ▶ **A few hundred paper clips**
- ▶ **Binder clips**
- ▶ **A trash can**
- ▶ **A paper shredder**
- ▶ **Bookshelves**
- ▶ **A filing cabinet (at least a two-drawer model)**

These items would replicate our home office, except we wouldn't have our own desks or desk chairs. Instead, I thought smugly, we'd each have our own deck chair—and a frozen cocktail with a little umbrella to make our tasks a little more bearable.

Then we took a serious look at the boat. The entire cabin interior was barely bigger than our home office, and it included a head and a galley. While our home office had at least eight electrical outlets (which I'd augmented with multi-input power strips so that we probably had fifteen to twenty cords plugged in at any given moment), the boat had only a couple of outlets. We were warned in the strongest possible terms against stringing together a half-dozen power strips and overloading the Cobalt's electrical system. An overloaded electrical system is a fire hazard (as evidenced by the rash of house fires each holiday season due to overloaded outlets bursting into flame), and an onboard electrical fire is more than a slight inconvenience. It was time to make a new list.

In order to make an onboard office work, even if you're going solo, you have to think creatively and spatially. Everything—and I mean everything—better be able to pull double or triple duty. One-use items are extravagances that cannot be afforded. Suddenly we went from being Mr. and Mrs. Santa Claus, ready to melt our American Express cards at the local electronics outlet, to being Mr. and Mrs. Hard-Nose, looking at every proposed item with a stern and demanding eye.

The entire cabin interior of a Cobalt 360 is barely bigger than a typical home office—with about twenty percent of the electrical outlets.

A navigator's desk like this is an excellent place for a laptop—but you'll still have to find storage for the rest of your electronic equipment.

WE GOT THE POWER

Even though we found plenty of fat to trim, many things were required and nonnegotiable. The computers, for example: There was no way we'd be able to share one computer. Luckily, that was the easiest obstacle to clear. Having spent my working life as a writer, and having been turned on to Apple's original Macintosh back in 1984, I wasn't going to give up my Mac now. Nor was Carey. In a bit of serendipitous timing, at the Macworld conference right before we decided to move onboard, Apple announced, in essence, that the desktop computer was a dinosaur and the company would be putting its energies into its notebook line. And so our computer troubles ended. I got a top-of-the-line PowerBook that weighed less than a pair of hiking boots and had more power and storage than any computer I'd ever owned. The 17-inch SuperDrive I bought came with a 17-inch display that wasn't much smaller than the flat-panel monitor I was using with my desktop computer, along with the ability to play and record both CDs and DVDs. Better still, the PowerBook came with wireless networking built in (both AirPort and Bluetooth) and an S-video output port to allow us to view DVDs on our television. This gave my PowerBook the ability to double as our DVD player, as long as we got a TV with an S-video input.

Carey opted for an iBook notebook with a 12.1-inch screen and a combination DVD/CD-RW drive, to which we added AirPort wireless networking. Compared to the iMac she'd been using, the iBook offered more memory, more power, and the ability to watch her own movies and burn her own CDs.

AT THE AIRPORT

The next step was to invest in an AirPort base station. Since my PowerBook and Carey's iBook had AirPort cards, the base station gave us full wireless networking capability, something essential to the success of our endeavor. (Without a network only one of us would be able to connect to the Internet at a time, a sure way to start at least seventeen fights per day.) With space onboard the Cobalt already at a premium, the last thing we wanted was wiring running everywhere.

Also, no matter how much you love somebody, you need elbow room. With a wireless network, we'd be able to work as closely as we wanted, or as far apart as the boat would allow. I could have my research papers scattered all over the cabin and be writing and e-mailing feverishly with CDs blasting through my headphones (which would be plugged into the PowerBook), while Carey could be surfing the Net and enjoying a warm, sunny afternoon up on the Cobalt's foredeck. In the best of all possible worlds, we could both be sitting topside, working or surfing the Net as we enjoyed a sunset, with the AirPort base station below, safely tucked away from the wind, sun, and any possible water.

THAT'S ENTERTAINMENT

Carey and I like how the PowerBook and iBook can double as personal entertainment centers if we choose. A set of headphones lets either of us enjoy a CD, a film on DVD, or even a collection of MP3s without bothering the other. This is more important than you may realize, especially if you and your partner have different work habits. If one of you can't work without music and the other can't work with anything but absolute silence, the built-in CD player on the notebook is a blessed peacemaker.

Your Friend, Duct Tape

This little trick will make your computer equipment significantly less vulnerable to water damage. (It has its limits, of course. If you drop your laptop into the ocean, you're on your own.)

1. Locate as many unused ports as you can on the computer, such as USB ports, the Ethernet jack, and the input jack for your power cord.

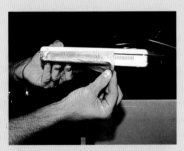

2. Cover them with duct tape.

3. Voilà! A valuable barrier to humidity, spills, and spray.

Incidentally, just because Carey and I are both members of the Cult of Macintosh when it comes to computers, doesn't mean PCs can't do the job. Here are some semi-equivalences:

APPLE	PC
▶ PowerBook	▶ Dell Inspiron 8500
▶ iBook	▶ Inspiron 600m
▶ AirPort	▶ D-Link Systems DWL-2000AP AirPlus Enhanced 2.4GHz Wireless Access Point

Any two notebooks that can be equipped with a wireless networking card (a feature of all new models today) and a wireless networking base station will work just fine.

KEEPING WATER AWAY

The important thing isn't whether you use Macs or PCs, but whether you can set up a wireless network. A wired network not only restricts your mobility and clutters the boat with cords and cables running everywhere, it's also much more susceptible to water damage. This is something you always have to be aware of when you're on a boat, even if that boat never leaves the dock. With a wireless network, you can actually take small pieces of duct tape and seal off your notebook computer's USB ports, serial ports (if it has serial ports), Ethernet ports, and power-input jack when you're above deck, almost eliminating the risk of water damage.

That very fear of water is why we invested in extra batteries for our PowerBook and iBook. With the extra batteries, if we began to run low on power while working above deck, we could just go below and put a fresh, charged battery in and get another four or five hours' worth of work done without needing to have the power cord connected to the computer up where water might be a problem. At night, we'd plug the computers in and charge the batteries. We could also work down in the cabin with the computer(s) plugged in and the batteries charging.

Waterproofing was also why we purchased carrying cases for both computers. Although the cases weren't completely watertight (they really shouldn't be, to prevent condensation within the case), they did let us cover up the computers at night, with the power cables plugged in, adding further protection from water or impacts. Your computer is your onboard livelihood, or lifeline, so you can't be obsessive enough about taking care of it.

Both our computers had built-in fax software and modems, which eliminated the need for a fax machine. By having the computer act as the fax, you can save your incoming faxes on CDs, putting hundreds on a single disk. You can even upload your digitally saved faxes, both incoming and outgoing, to an FTP site. You can also use this to back up all your computer's files.

Having neatly disposed of our need for a fax machine, thereby saving space and freeing up at least one electrical outlet, we turned our attention to the next item on our office need/want list: the printer. Try as we might, we've still not reached that paperless nirvana the computer folks have been promising. We need a printer. So we decided we might as well have a decent one that can do a passable job of printing photographs. We also decided that we'd take at least a baby step toward that paperless future and get an all-in-one printer/scanner/copier. That way, if someone sent us a document we might need in the future but not something so critical we'd ever need it in a court of law, we could scan it, save it digitally to a CD, and toss the paper. The color copier function is a bonus.

There are enough all-in-ones out there to fill a catalog. We chose an Epson Stylus CX5200, which prints respectably (5760 x 1440 optimized dpi) at a decent speed (twenty-two pages per minute if you're only printing black text) and copies at a fair clip (fifteen copies per minute for black text only). When you're not in an office, blazing speed isn't usually the most important aspect of your printer or copier. Nobody's standing over your shoulder, tapping feet and jingling pocket change, trying to get you to hurry up. So the Epson does fine for us.

The Epson is compatible with both Macs and PCs. Even better is that it's a printer with a USB connection, so we could plug it into our AirPort base station and Carey and I could both use it without having to swap cables or any of that nonsense. And it's small enough—17.8" x 17.1" x 10", with trays extended—and weighs only 20 pounds (including ink cartridges), so it can be easily stowed when we're not using it. Actually,

Of Windows and Portholes

Windows die-hards can set up onboard computer systems equivalent to an Apple-based one. For example, you could use the following hardware:

- A higher-end notebook such as Dell's Inspiron 8500
- A lower-end notebook such as Dell's Inspiron 600m
- D-Link's DWL-2000AP wireless networking station

TIP

It's important to remember that not all cellular providers support all phones—so if you have your heart set on one specific model, you may need to shop around for the cellular provider that's best for you.

we stowed it even when we *were* using it, completely out of sight in a closet with the AirPort base station.

IT'S FOR YOU (OR IS IT?)

Another must-have is a telephone. Deciding what kind of phone—and which service—was easier once we'd decided to live on Lake Travis instead of the coast. Had we chosen the coastal home port, the possibility of going offshore more than a few miles, maybe even for more than a few days, starts increasing. But as you go farther offshore, cellular service seriously decreases—down to zip, in fact. At that point, you have to start looking beyond cellular service and toward satellite telephones.

Satellite phones have had a rough time so far. The best-known service, Iridium, has gone in and out of business repeatedly. However, KVH (*www.kvh.com*) has a satellite phone that works well: the Tracphone 252. It's a single-cable, self-contained model that can even be plugged into a computer for dial-up Internet access. Of course, at $1.95 per minute, you'll pay so much for that connection you'll rue the day you ever heard of the Internet or satellite telephones. The Tracphone 252 does work well for sending and receiving faxes, though, as well as for voice calls. (You'll just have to learn to speak quickly.)

However, because we weren't going offshore, Carey and I really had no need for satellite telephone service. Cellular gave us the ability to have two dedicated phone lines at a reasonable price and with reasonable coverage. We already had one cell phone, so we'd have to get a second. I'd had a Nokia phone with AT&T Wireless service for years, and had never had a complaint, so we initially thought we'd get another Nokia. Then I discovered that the Motorola T721 phone had a USB data connector accessory, which would give us the ability to plug the phone directly into our computers to send and receive faxes. It was settled. We'd get one of those.

SURFING: CELL OR SATELLITE?

We could also use the Motorola T721 for dial-up Internet access. However, if you're accustomed to broadband Internet access (as we were), dial-up can be frustrating. For one thing, it ties up your phone. For another, it's so slow that you will go stark raving mad.

We were spoiled, having had broadband at the home office for years. We wanted it onboard, too. The problem is, broadband Internet access is generally available only as a wired service. DSL runs on telephone landlines, and cable runs on fiber-optic cable that also carries TV service. So we turned to satellite Internet access, the same technology that delivers TV service.

Only a few years ago, satellite TV was the domain of rural types and hardcore media geeks who didn't mind putting 12-foot-diameter dishes in their yards to pull in signals. However, in 2003, if you drive by an apartment building almost anywhere in the United States you see dozens of mini-dishes pulling in Dish Network and DirecTV. The same thing is starting to happen with Internet access. Providers like Earthlink and AOL are offering broadband Internet connectivity via satellite, and I won't be surprised if that becomes the connection of choice before very long.

The drawback with satellite Internet service is that the dish has to be aimed right at the satellite. This isn't a problem at a house, which stays in the same place. The Cobalt 360, however, was going to be mobile. I suppose I could've gone Rube Goldberg in this situation, rigging up a system of electric motors and drive belts that I'd be able to operate remotely to adjust the antenna while we were under way in a ridiculous effort to keep our Internet connection up and running. A more realistic but much more expensive option was to spend a ton of money to order TracNet 2.0 Internet service from KVH.

TracNet 2.0 delivers download speeds of 400 Kbps and is even equipped with 802.11b wireless technology. If we had wanted, we could have done without the AirPort base station. TracNet's big selling point was its ability to stay connected not just wherever we docked, but even while we were under way. Carey could check her e-mail while I motored us up the lake, or I could surf the Web while she was at the helm. But that kind of benefit doesn't come cheap.

When I priced TracNet (in Spring 2003), the retail price was $5,995, plus monthly access, which ranged from $190 per month for 250 minutes of Internet connection (about 76 cents per minute) up to $490 per

Satellite Savvy

KVH's satellite telephone (the Tracphone 252, above) and broadband Internet (TracNet 2.0, below) services can follow you virtually anywhere you go—but this kind of convenience doesn't come cheap.

month for 1,500 minutes of Internet connection (about 33 cents per minute; every minute past 1,500 charged at 69 cents per minute). There was also a plan available where we would pay $99 per month for connectivity, plus 99 cents per minute. Figure that out: With 1,500 minutes and a thirty-day month, we would get only fifty minutes on-line per day. Because I do so much research on the Internet, that would be impossible for me.

We decided instead that each of us would get a Motorola T721 cell phone with USB connection and a calling plan that would feature unlimited night and weekend minutes. During the day, we could connect to the Internet briefly to check our e-mail (or even use the phones' e-mail capability). At night we'd do our research and Web surfing. This would take some adjustment, but the cost savings would be worthwhile. Since we would be on a lake in a semi-urban area and our computers would be equipped with AirPort cards, we would be able to take

Depending on the sort of boat you want, and the sort of life you want to lead, you can find all the office space you need. This man is a computer consultant and webmaster who runs a full-fledged office from aboard his restored canal barge.

advantage of wireless Internet access points offered at many hotels and coffee shops. (Some marinas are now also offering WiFi Internet access.)

TV OR NOT TV

Then it was time to choose our television service. KVH's TracVision C3, a satellite service, not only can receive DirecTV from any marina slip or dock, it can also pull in DirecTV while you're under way, or even if you're anchored out in the middle of nowhere. Carey doesn't watch a lot of television, but she does love movies and she's hooked on certain HBO series. Personally, I couldn't live without ESPN for baseball and FOX Sports World for international rugby coverage, so we had to have satellite service.

The TracVision C3 had, at the time, a retail price of $3,495 (not including installation), which is a lot of money for a satellite receiver. But the resale value of the Cobalt 360 would be substantially increased by the addition of the TracVision C3, so we felt it would be a justifiable expense.

The Cobalt 360 had a built-in TV/VCR combo as an option. As a built-in unit, the combo would already be installed and would be included in the Cobalt's warranty. Combined with the TracVision C3, the built-in TV/VCR combo unit would increase the resale value of the boat a little bit. (Any option helps with the resale value, so it pays to get a boat that's absolutely loaded.)

Of course, many people manage to live and work onboard very well without a TV at all. Tom MacNaughton told me, "The idea that happiness afloat will consist of making your boat as much like a house ashore as possible will never work. You must simplify. Think Thoreau. Admire the Amish ideals of simple, plain, natural living without pride or show but with frugality and thrift. Reduce your wants and you will increase your happiness."

Daisy Garnett, a freelance writer, echoed Tom's sentiments when she told the *New York Times* about a transatlantic sail: "I became smug about how both spartan and unspartan our life at sea was. We did without telephones or newspapers or freshwater shower or video games or DVDs, and yet we ate hot meals and had a library of books to read."

But Carey and I didn't want to simplify that much. We considered giving up the TV and the TracVision, but because I was now working in the medium, I was able to convince her to keep them. We never, however, considered doing without a radio.

RADIO: CATCHING THE WAVES

Satellites are changing the way we listen to radio. Picking up radio stations has traditionally been a problem onboard. The frequency bands, AM and FM, have severe technical limitations. Without getting into too much detail, AM (Amplitude Modulation) is based on the height of the radio waves, while FM (Frequency Modulation) is based on how many wave peaks occur in a given time period. Of the two, AM is much more powerful but much more low-fidelity, thus susceptible to interference from such electrical impulses as lightning and overhead power lines. FM is substantially more high-fidelity, with clearer reception and much less static and interference, but much more limited by transmission distance, so it's rare to pick up an FM station more than 75 miles from its broadcast antenna. Also if there are many hills or mountains between you and the antenna, reception and broadcast quality will be further reduced.

(Shortwave radio has been a marine standby for years, allowing you to listen to stations from around the world. Shortwave is great for hearing weird stuff from other countries, but it's not very good for accessing local stations, because the physics of shortwave broadcasting makes local reception spotty at best. Some decent shortwave receivers are available, but most shortwave enthusiasts use large, fairly expensive receivers and antennae. If you're going to be doing long-distance, offshore cruising—to the Caribbean for example—then a shortwave receiver would probably be a worthwhile investment.)

In sum, boats are just about the worst possible candidates for decent radio reception, because so many of the most popular waterways, especially lakes, are miles from population centers and are often surrounded by hills or mountains. Offshore is just as bad. Radio broadcasters, well aware of how few people live in the middle of the ocean, tend to put their antennae miles and miles inland, so usually the signal barely extends beyond the coastline. Boaters generally have to make do with either poor reception or reliance on tape decks and CD players to make music.

The trouble is, if you drop a tape or a CD overboard, it will sink. To leave either out in the direct sunlight is to cause electronic mayhem. And so with these factors in mind, satellite radio comes charging in like the cavalry.

As of this writing, there are two satellite radio services available in the United States: XM and Sirius. They work using the same basic technology. XM, for example, has two satellites ("Rock" and "Roll") in geosynchronous orbit over the United States. Each is stationed about 22,000 miles above ground: one on the East Coast, and one on the West. Since the satellites stay fixed in position, their 10-megawatt transmissions cover all forty-eight contiguous states, including offshore and into Canada and Mexico. Equipped with a special antenna and receiver, you can receive virtually CD-quality, digital audio broadcasts anywhere in the United States.

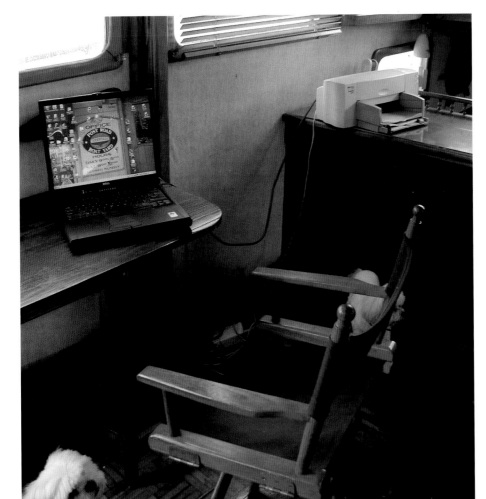

Kent Doyle's office was a self-installation project. Electricity comes from a bank of batteries.

You don't only get digital audio that's all but indistinguishable from CDs. You also get it without static or interference, and you get it anywhere you go. With satellite radio, you can pick a station when you board your boat in Key West and never have to change it, even if you go all the way to Portland, Maine—or Portland, Oregon.

If you want to listen to talk radio instead of music, you can. Both XM and Sirius offer a number of satellite stations that broadcast nothing but talk, all day, all night, in stereo. The fact is, with satellite radio you can choose from more than 100 stations, just like cable or satellite TV, with stations primed to fit into just about every imaginable niche. And you can't overestimate the added peace of mind you get from having the ability to dial in The Weather Channel anytime, anywhere, to get updates and information on what's going on, especially during the more active weather seasons.

Although Carey and I already owned a Delphi SkyFi boom box, a portable XM radio receiver, we ordered the optional XM package Cobalt offers on the 360. This would, once again, drive up the resale value and eliminate any installation hassles, which were becoming an issue.

DO IT YOURSELF (OR NOT)

When we first started putting our onboard office together, I fantasized that I'd be able to do all the installations myself. Even though experience and evidence point to the contrary, I like to think of myself as a highly skilled handyman, a sort of MacGyver, who can make almost anything work. I really am good at following instructions once I get around to reading them, so it seemed like self-installation would be a good idea. We were spending a lot of money on this gear, and self-installation would save a few bucks. On top of that, by doing it myself I'd understand how everything worked. If we ever encountered any problems, I'd be ready and able to deal with them instead of having to call the service technician.

Carey saw things differently. She agreed that we were spending a lot of money on our equipment, and that we were planning to relocate and continue to use most, if not all of it, in our house when and if our liveaboard adventure was finished. But her conclusion was different: it was more important than ever that we have everything professionally installed. That way we'd know the job had been done right, or at least have a guarantee that the installer would fix or pay for anything broken during the process, and that everything would work when it was all completed as planned.

I pointed out that eventually I got everything I'd ever installed to work, and that I had fixed or paid for anything that was damaged during the installation process. I pointed out that living and working onboard is an act of self-sufficiency, that we were proving we could go it alone, and that by paying for professional installation we'd be sacrificing that self-sufficiency. I also pointed out that there's an immense self-gratification that comes from doing this kind of thing, where you attack a job and knock it out, thus proving your abilities. As far as I was concerned, this self-satisfaction, along with the tangential bonuses of knowing how everything worked and how everything was put in place, far outweighed everything else. I wanted to feel as though (as Kent Doyle told *The New York Times*), "This boat runs because I make it run."

Carey was not swayed. She reminded me that self-installation, even for someone more mechanically inclined than I, is a long process. You have to cut holes, run wires, test things. She said that's why there are people who work full-time installing things like satellite antennas and television hookups on boats: It's a full-time job. Since I already had a job, I'd have the choice between doing the installations in my spare time—an hour or so per day (if that) during the week and a bit more on weekends—which would make the process even more drawn-out, or essentially blowing off my real job and going full-time into the installation process. That would not have a very beneficial impact on our financial situation.

This is the sort of discussion that can and will erupt with increasing frequency as you get ready to start your onboard adventure. I use the word "erupt" because these discussions can quickly go from "You know, love, I was thinking maybe we ought to save some money, and I kind of want to anyway, so I'll just do it all myself...." to "You couldn't install a roll of toilet paper without professional help...." and then on to expletives and guttural screams. If building a 3,000-square-foot dream house can wreck a marriage or partnership, so can moving onboard a 36-foot boat.

TIP

Installing it all yourself is cheaper than calling in the pros, and the act of self-sufficiency is seductive. But it requires time and expertise—and if you're not sure you have enough of each, you may wish to reconsider.

In talking with people before taking on this project, I'd been warned about the tension and stress that would inevitably arise. Carey and I had each vowed that when things started getting heated over what was really an inconsequential issue, such as whether to install everything myself or have it done professionally, we'd break away from the whole thing for a day or so and come back with cooler heads. It was a tip my father had given me, and it worked.

After a couple days' thought on the subject, and some intense discussion with Clayton Raven at Boat Town, Kent Bridges in Redwood City, and a few others, I came to understand that installing electronic gear like the TracVision antenna and wiring it up is a lot more involved than I'd realized. It's not like installing a satellite dish at your house, in which you simply drill in some screws for the mount, get out your compass to align the dish, drill a hole in the wall to pass the cable through, caulk up said hole, plug the cable into the dish receiver, and you're in business.

Installing the TracVision antenna involved mounting the unit on the Cobalt's "radar arch," running cable through the arch and the gunwale, then installing a cable outlet in the interior wall where we were planning to keep the receiver. This wasn't a simple job, and I finally agreed with Carey that the best plan would be to have the system professionally installed.

There are several things to consider when choosing do-it-yourself or professional installation, but first and foremost, you always, always have to think about water and its effect on equipment. Few things, in fact, are more detrimental to the performance of an electronic component than water, especially salt water. If you're in a saltwater environment, you'll have to go three miles past obsessive to even find the starting point for your fanaticism about keeping your equipment high and dry.

GO WITH THE PROS

That said, an even stronger reason for choosing professional installation remained. Professionals understand the marine environment and how incompatible it is with our electronic lifestyle, and they know how to make the two mesh. If you do your research and ask any potential installer for references, and then check those references, you can almost guarantee yourself a quality piece of work. That quality will include ensuring that every hull installation is cleanly and solidly sealed. The same applies for the interior installations. You can do this yourself, but you have to be obsessively attentive to detail.

So we decided the TracVision system would be professionally installed but everything else would be installed by me. All decisions on placement were based first on practicality, second on common consent with Carey. Actually, as is the case with most office equipment, installation was little more than plugging stuff into electrical outlets.

Set up your office to take advantage of whatever storage facilities you have. Keeping printers, outlets, and cables tucked away in cabinets like the ones here keeps them safely out of harm's way.

> Wireless is a godsend if you're going to be working onboard. If we hadn't gone wireless, we'd never have lasted a single weekend.

Since we'd gone wireless with our AirPort networking, the only cable that I had to deal with was the one connecting our printer/scanner to the AirPort base station.

Wireless is a godsend if you're going to be working onboard. It gives you mobility and security in terms of avoiding water, which is a real concern. If you're hardwired onboard, you'll probably have to set up the equivalent of a traditional desk and office using the dining table as your desk. But actually, even if you're wireless you may find yourself working this way a lot. Let's face it: we've all spent the vast majority of our working lives at a desk, and that's how we're most comfortable working. The difference is, if you're wired, you don't have any choice in the matter. You can't leave. And even if you have a great air conditioner on your boat, you won't want to spend every working day stuck down in the cabin in the aquatic equivalent of a cubicle.

Kent Bridges told me he lived onboard for a year or more without ever setting up an office on his boat in San Francisco Bay. It was too confining, he said, working down in the cabin every day. Kent's a country boy at heart, having grown up on a ranch and still raising horses, so being locked within four walls, even with a view of the bay and a refrigerator full of Sonoma County chardonnays, is anathema to him. So he'd live onboard and still commute to an office to do his work. "Too cramped," he said with a shrug when I asked him about working onboard for an extended period. "It's okay if I have some papers to read at night after dinner or a couple of e-mails to write so I can send 'em out first thing when I get to the office or the airport, but other than that, I can't work here."

I am a cave dweller by nature, a lover of low ceilings and dark spaces. Still, Kent's words stuck with me as I looked long and hard at the Cobalt 360's cabin and tried to imagine working in there most of every day. It started to look very, very small.

Carey is my polar opposite when it comes to caves. She verges on claustrophobic. So she finds the notion of being cooped up in the cabin of any boat this side of a Princess cruise ship unnerving. The idea of the two of us wired to each other and the Internet connection and the printer/scanner, as well as having the dogs and the cat in the Cobalt's cabin for more than a few hours at a time, didn't sit well with us at all. If we hadn't gone wireless, we'd have never spent a single weekend living and working onboard that boat.

To prepare ourselves for working in close quarters, the last thing we did before we moved onboard was to spend a couple of weeks doing a land-based "shakedown cruise." We started tearing down our home office to replicate the onboard office as closely as possible to see what we had overlooked, if anything.

I highly recommend the home-office test. Use a bedroom that closely approximates the size of your boat's cabin, excluding the midcabin berth or staterooms (if you have them on your boat). Use chairs, desks, bookshelves or whatever else is available to replicate the cabin's interior, with seating along the V-berth, a galley, and so forth. Then introduce your new office equipment to that space. Whatever you're thinking of bringing onboard, bring into your test office. And if it's not going to be onboard, it needs to be out of the office and off-limits unless absolutely necessary. Then spend a week working in the test office. You're allowed to sleep in another room, but only if you have a midcabin berth or staterooms on your boat. If not, you also have to sleep in the office. This is a real eye-opener.

THE DAILY GRIND

The first thing most people discover is that they need a coffeemaker. Carey and I had been so focused on the sexier stuff like computers and televisions that we'd completely forgotten to include one. So we moved a coffeemaker into the home office within five minutes of starting our shakedown cruise.

The second thing we discovered is that living out of an ice chest is okay when you're nineteen and on spring break, but when you're an adult you want a refrigerator, even if it takes up precious office space. The Cobalt 360 does have a refrigerator, but it's a small one. Carey and I only allowed ourselves to put as much in our full-size home refrigerator as we would be able to fit into the Cobalt's fridge. That wasn't much. Constant, mindless snacking would become pretty much impossible onboard because there's just not enough room to store junk food.

Aside from the coffeemaker and refrigerator, though, it turned out we'd done a pretty good job in equipping our office. The computers worked well, and the AirPort did the job of networking the computers and the printer/scanner. The lack of wires and cables was cause for celebration. The close quarters of the bedroom posed no major problems, and the dogs all seemed more than happy to lie around at our feet. We just got used to stepping over them. Scanning and shredding papers was working out okay, although it was more of a hassle than anticipated to get a CD, fire it up, and open a file when all we wanted was a phone number.

The biggest discovery of the shakedown cruise was how little of the space in our house we actually use. Everyone, it seems, is always talking about how they need more room and are looking for a bigger house. A 1,500-square foot house is considered small; a 2,000-square foot house is cramped; and a 2,500-square foot house is about the minimum people seem to be looking for these days, even if they live alone. Yet what Carey and I found, as we essentially locked ourselves in the home office, was that we appreciate the space of our house but don't really use it. And that was almost exactly what Kent Bridges had told me he'd discovered when he moved onboard. The lack of space is noticeable, but it doesn't have much of an impact on your life. It's different, of course, if you have a family, because each person physically takes up a certain amount of space. The more people there are onboard, the more they're going to be bumping into each other.

Even with just two people onboard, much less two people and three dogs, you have to learn to dance together in order to move easily around any confined space, whether on a boat or on land. This is another thing we'd been warned about, and one that the at-home shakedown cruise put into sharp relief. A good bit of advice I picked up from Stan Wasilewsky by way of the IRBS liveaboard e-mail list (archived at *www.irbs.com/lists/live-aboard*) is this: "Bite the bullet and rent a 30- or 32-foot travel trailer (RV) for about six months. That will allow you to test the water, so to speak, to see if you and your (partner) can live together in those confining quarters."

That also has the benefit of showing you just how much of your stuff you'll have to do without for the duration of your living and working onboard adventure. You'll have to give up more or less all of your furniture and almost all your clothes, which can be traumatic if you or your partner is the sentimental type who needs and wants certain mementos around. "My wife loved our dining room set," Stan writes, "and cried when we sold it."

Most important, we found that our selection of equipment and supplies covered all our needs, except for the coffeemaker issue. There was no unnecessary equipment, either. We used everything and never went looking for anything else during our test phase, so we were ready for the final steps in preparing the office: protecting the equipment.

Having your electronic equipment carefully installed and keeping that equipment as safe as possible in the cabin greatly reduces the risk of exposure to moisture. But impact and jostling are larger concerns than moisture, unless you never leave the dock. As you motor across even relatively smooth water, the equipment down below can take a real beating. Any sudden changes of direction will toss your equipment about, even if the location is a closet. Most of the equipment onboard, especially the items that were either factory standard or professionally installed, will have been designed to withstand some jostling and banging. But computers, printers, scanners, and fax machines aren't usually built to handle such rough treatment.

TIP

However your equipment gets installed, the installation should focus on avoiding two things: moisture and jostling.

AN OUNCE OF PROTECTION

There's a simple, effective way to protect that equipment. First, go to the local camping supply store (REI, for instance) and purchase some egg-crate mattress foam. (This is also available at mattress outlets.) It should be at least an inch thick. While you're at the camping store, purchase about six foot-long bungee cords. Then go to the hardware store and buy a dozen small (half-inch eyelet) screw-in eyehooks and some super glue.

Cut the egg-crate foam to fit the bottom and interior side walls and door of the closet or wherever your electronics will be stored. Glue the foam in place. Place the equipment in the position you want it. Screw in an eyehook a couple of inches from each corner of the piece of equipment. Then use the bungee cords to secure the equipment. Now you have your electronics on a nice padded surface, which when bouncing will be cushioned against impact. The elastic bungee cords will hold the equipment in place in all but the most severe maneuvers.

I picked that last tip up by hanging around marinas and checking out the liveaboards there. Another tip I picked up by walking around with my eyes and ears open is that a small, rechargeable, handheld vacuum like Black & Decker's Dustbuster is something you must have onboard, as is a small electric-broom vacuum. Use them to keep sand and dirt from beaches and docksides from building up inside the cabin. (The Dustbuster is also a good way to clean out your notebook's keyboard.)

The last great tip I picked up around the docks is to invest in rechargeable batteries—twice as many as you need to run everything that takes batteries—and a recharger. The rechargeables are more expensive than regular batteries, but over time they'll pay for themselves. More important, by having twice as many as you need, you can always keep a full supply of charged batteries onboard so you'll never find yourself stuck without batteries. Nor will you be constantly buying batteries at exorbitant marina prices. Store extra batteries in the boat's refrigerator, where humidity is lowest on the boat—this helps avoid corrosion.

You can get incredibly bogged down in the minutiae of setting up

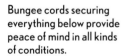

Bungee cords securing everything below provide peace of mind in all kinds of conditions.

your onboard office. But everything reaches a point of diminishing returns, where you're doing a lot of work in exchange for little real benefit. When you've reached the battery stage, you're at that point. It's time to do the real thing.

Double-check that you have what you need:

▶ **Computer(s) that can pull double duty as a fax machine, triple duty as a personal CD player, and quadruple duty as a DVD player so you can watch movies on the computer screen**

▶ **A wireless networking system**

▶ **A cell phone that can connect to your computer to enable fax capabilities**

▶ **Internet access, either via satellite, cell phone, or landline at the marina**

▶ **A small-footprint, all-in-one printer/scanner/copier**

▶ **CDs for storing your documents and a paper shredder to get rid of printed documents**

▶ **An at-home shakedown cruise to make sure you can get by comfortably with the bare minimum of equipment and supplies, and that you're not forgetting anything**

Now you're ready.

TIP

Invest in rechargeable batteries and a recharger.

CHAPTER 5

ADJUSTING TO LIFE ONBOARD

MOVING ONBOARD IS KIND OF LIKE THE FIRST TIME YOU MOVE OUT OF YOUR PARENTS' HOUSE. IT'S EXCITING. EVERYTHING'S DIFFERENT. IT'S ALSO KIND OF LIKE GOING ON HOLIDAY. YOU'RE STAYING IN A SMALLER SPACE THAN YOU'RE ACCUSTOMED TO, BUT IT'S EXOTIC AND THEREFORE OKAY.

You're filled with all kinds of fantasies about what life onboard will be like. You'll fall asleep on the foredeck watching meteor showers. You'll wake to the sun rising and the sound of water lapping against the hull. You'll be more productive than ever in your entire life. You'll be a captain of industry (like Bill Gates, but richer) when you're not writing best-selling and incredibly deep, thoughtful, literary novels (like Hemingway, but more sober). You might even direct a few independent films. The world, you think, will be your oyster.

Carey and Dave Kelley relax in the cockpit of their boat.

CONTENTS

- ▶ *What* Closet Space?
- ▶ Weather Watch
- ▶ Galley Gear
- ▶ Forming Onboard Habits

There's a fair amount of storage in this bedroom—by a boater's standards. Note cabinets built into base of bed.

Then you move aboard, and reality hits you like a train.

The first smack your skull gets is when you start comparing the closet space onboard your boat to the closet space in your house. As Kent Doyle says of his boat, "there's sleeping room for six people and storage room for 0.4." Carey and I figured we were losing at least 95 percent of our closet space—not counting dressers and chests-of-drawers—before we had the bright idea of putting the printer/scanner and AirPort base station in the closet. That's right. *The* closet. On land, Carey and I had two and a half closets each. Onboard the Cobalt 360, we shared one closet with each other and a couple of pieces of office equipment.

Of course, you need very few items of clothing to live and work onboard successfully, even if you'll be onboard for a really long time. T-shirts, shorts, swimsuits, deck shoes, and sandals are the primary attire of liveaboards. Why not? Who's looking? Plus, those are all items that can be folded so that they take up very little onboard storage space.

Because you won't be able to fit much onboard, everyone goes through the "winnowing of the wardrobe." Once again, Kent Bridges was my mentor, and his advice was excellent: Keep only what you'll wear, and keep only half of that.

Carey and I took a wardrobe that was pretty basic. We each brought:

- ▶ **Six short-sleeved T-shirts**
- ▶ **Six long-sleeved Ts**
- ▶ **Three polo shirts**
- ▶ **One fleece pullover**
- ▶ **One pair of jeans**
- ▶ **One pair of khakis**
- ▶ **One pair of sweat pants**
- ▶ **Three pairs of running socks**
- ▶ **One pair of running shoes**
- ▶ **One pair of dress shoes and socks to match (for me)**
- ▶ **One pair of deck shoes**
- ▶ **One pair of sandals**
- ▶ **One set of foul-weather gear**

For business meetings or other occasions, I brought a suit and Carey brought a dress. I brought three pairs of running shorts that could double as swim trunks and three pairs of rugby shorts. Carey brought two swimsuits and three pairs of khaki shorts, as well as two sets of running gear—shorts and sports bras. We also brought baseball caps and wide-brimmed hats.

DOUBLE-DUTY DUDS

We planned the wardrobe to exceed slightly our minimal anticipated needs. As with the office equipment, we also tried to make sure what we brought could pull double duty. We both run for mental and physical health, so we needed the appropriate gear, all of which could double as swim gear or just hanging-out clothing. The long-sleeved Ts were needed because even in the brutal heat of August in Texas, it can get downright chilly at night if you're in the middle of a lake with a breeze coming off the water. In cooler seasons, we'd be able to use the long-sleeved Ts for working out and even to layer with the short-sleeves and the fleece pullovers.

We planned on wearing swimsuits as standard, everyday gear while on the boat. We figured as long as we kept ourselves slathered in SPF45 sunblock and spent most of our time in the shade of the Bimini top, we'd

Kent Doyle stores his shoes on an unused ladder to save space.

be safe from the sun. And when the sun set, we could add a T-shirt and shorts or sweat pants.

The jeans and khaki trousers would be onboard in case the weather turned nippy or we decided to leave the boat for dinner and visit a restaurant that required long pants. The polo shirts would come in handy in those situations, too, and could also be worn comfortably onboard. Deck shoes can be worn anywhere and look pretty swell with khaki trousers.

The only wardrobe items that would be single-purpose—and worn, really, as infrequently as possible—would be the foul-weather gear, my suit, and Carey's dress. Even for important meetings, though, you can, of course, get by without a suit. Kent Doyle swears by his blue blazer. Over a polo shirt, worn with a pair of khaki trousers and deck shoes, a blazer gives you a dashing sort of New England preppy air. Women can get away with that look, too—okay, maybe not the polo, but a blazer, blouse, and khakis look pretty sharp.

I went with the full blue suit because a suit will get you in anywhere, and in a pinch you can wear the suit jacket as a blazer with your polo and khakis. Besides, the suit, and the dress shirt, tie, and belt that go with it, take up exactly the same amount of space as a blazer—one hanger. Carey's confidence in the ability of the classic "little black dress" to fit any and all occasions is unbounded, so she chose that instead of dressing as my doppelganger.

So we wound up with a wardrobe that required as little as one hanger apiece, with the rest of our clothing able to be folded and stowed in drawers, along with our shoes.

The fact that we were going to be in Austin, where as a rule there are fewer than a dozen freezes a year, and temperatures that hover in the "T-shirt and shorts" comfort zone for more than ten months made our wardrobe choices considerably easier than if we were in a less boating-friendly climate. Austin's laid-back atmosphere helped, too, as there are few meetings, events, or restaurants that require more than the basic "shoes and shirt" wardrobe. Around these parts, it's possible to go your whole life without ever having to wear anything fancier than a polo shirt and a pair of khaki trousers.

Envisioning the places you wish to visit will help you to plan your onboard wardrobe.

Wardrobe Checklist: Summer

▶ Swimsuits

▶ Deck shoes

▶ T-shirts, both short-sleeved and long-sleeved

▶ Shorts

▶ Polo shirts

▶ Sandals

▶ Blazer and khaki trousers for men

▶ Cocktail dress or blazer, khakis, and shirt for women

▶ Suit for men

▶ Evening dress for women if needed

▶ Workout gear as appropriate

▶ Fleece pullover or sweats

▶ Foul-weather gear

Wardrobe Checklist: Winter

► Fleece pullover or sweats

► T-shirts

► Socks

► Sweaters

► Pea coat or other water-resistant heavy coat

► Deck shoes

► Blazer and khaki trousers for men

► Cocktail dress or blazer, khakis, and shirt for women

► Suit for men

► Evening dress for women if needed

► Workout gear as appropriate

► Foul weather gear

Miami is temperate enough for T-shirt and shorts, but to venture out into the Miami nightlife is to strut with the peacocks. You may want to stock your wardrobe with suits and outfits that will be acceptable attire for the restaurants and clubs in the area. New York requires dressing up for going out, as well as planning for lots and lots of cool-to-cold weather. Kent Doyle keeps an ancillary storage unit for winter clothes. Donna Emmons, who lives onboard a Hunter 31 sailboat at a New England marina, only keeps a week's worth of clothes onboard at a time, with the rest either at the laundry or in storage.

San Francisco is pretty easygoing about wardrobe, but the constant chill winds that blow off the Pacific and the Bay are why Mark Twain's comment about a summer in San Francisco being the coldest winter of his life still rings true. That's also why Kent Bridges' wardrobe onboard his Chris-Craft in San Francisco Bay is filled to bursting with fleece pullovers and other cool-weather gear.

If you intend to live and work for a long period in an area with well-defined seasons, like most anywhere along the Mississippi River north of Louisiana, it's a good idea to follow the lead of Kent Doyle and Donna Emmons and invest in a land-based clothing storage space. That way, you can stash your summer gear safely over the winter and vice-versa.

WEATHER OR NOT

"Weather becomes an obsession onboard."

Carey and I wouldn't have to worry about cold weather much, but we would have to worry about storms, especially in spring. If you spend time on a boat anywhere, sooner or later you'll get caught in the rain.

Even if your boat is just a floating apartment, you really should invest in good foul-weather gear. You hope you never need to put it on, but if the need arises, you'll be glad it's there. It's not cheap, but it can last for years if you take good care of it. Carey and I bought our gear from West Marine's online store (*www.westmarine.com*). We each got an Explorer breathable bib and an Explorer breathable jacket. The breathable aspect is important, because nonbreathable foul-weather gear, which is dramatically cheaper to buy, is essentially an airtight rubber suit that can make you feel like you're wearing a plastic trash bag. It gets hot, and then you get sweaty. The Explorer gear, on the other hand, has a microporous coating so that moisture on the inside (your sweat) can escape to the outside, but moisture on the outside (the rain) can't get in.

The bib is like a rainproof set of overalls, with Lycra suspenders and neoprene leg cuffs for a tight seal. The bib can work fine alone if you're doing some wade fishing (always be on the lookout for the double-duty), but in a real downpour you'll need to add the jacket. Like the bib, the jacket needs breathability. It should also have a high collar and a stowaway hood (the hood rolls up into a pocket on the jacket's collar). Pockets are good to have. More important, though, is that the jacket has highly reflective tape on the sleeves and torso, so you can be seen when visibility is poor.

Some people recommended the super-high-tech, foul-weather gear that comes with built-in flotation. If we were going coastal, we'd probably have opted for that. There are so many more variables in coastal weather that you have to take more into account

Squalls can strike with little notice. Be ready with the right gear.

TIP

Bookmark the best of the weather websites to keep on top of the latest conditions.

than if you're inland. Living and working on Lake Travis meant that we could expect enough warning of potentially dangerous weather to get to a more protected marina or off the lake entirely. Also, it meant that if we did get caught in a sudden storm, we'd still have time to put on a personal flotation device over or under our foul-weather jacket.

Weather becomes an obsession when you start living and working onboard, even if it's just for a weekend at a time. Obsession may even be too weak a word. I've heard on more than one occasion of liveaboards who didn't know about the terrorist attacks of September 11, 2001 for days because their onboard radios were permanently tuned to the NOAA (National Oceanic and Atmospheric Administration) weather broadcasts. These stories may be apocryphal, but I do know that if you spend any time on the water, you'll become a full-fledged weather geek.

There's a good reason for this weathercentric mindset. Bad weather can be a nuisance in everyday life, but to a boater, it can be life-threatening. As soon as you've white-knuckled your way through a two-hour squall, with 50-mph winds and driving rain that caught you off guard because you went out without checking the weather, you'll understand.

But modern technology has made weather geekdom easily attainable. You can dial in The Weather Channel on DirecTV or the Dish Network and keep tabs on conditions all day long. Many websites deliver constantly updated weather conditions, forecasts, and warnings. Weather radios stay tuned to NOAA at all times. Some weather radios automatically turn on whenever NOAA broadcasts a severe weather alert. It can actually seem as if it's harder not to know what the weather's going to be than it is to stay informed.

STORM WATCH

A weather radio is sufficient for most inland conditions, so long as you keep the batteries charged. In my experience, though, once you start actually living and working out in the weather instead of in a climate-controlled office, you really do start watching The Weather Channel more than anything else on TV. You also start bookmarking the best of the

L to R: Nimbus, cumulus and stratus clouds. Learning to read the skies can keep you from nasty surprises.

weather websites (like *www.weather.com* and *www.weather.gov*) so you can stay apprised of developing situations. There are also a few computer applications that keep weather conditions, forecasts, and alerts constantly on your desktop as long as you have an "always on" Internet connection (such as satellite broadband or WiFi). Carey and I installed WeatherManX on our Macs, available from AfterTen Software (*www.afterten.com*). This program puts the current conditions on the menu bar and with one mouse click will direct us to the National Weather Service website whenever severe weather alerts are issued. It's indispensable. Windows users can get the WeatherBug (*www.weatherbug.com*), which does virtually the same things.

No matter which official communications you can tap into, you should learn to read the skies and weather charts yourself. That way you can have an idea of what's going on meteorologically and feel more connected to your surroundings. If you're in coastal waters, it's an even better idea.

Reading the weather isn't all that difficult. The first rule of thumb is that in North America, weather generally moves from west to east. So pay extra attention to what's happening in the west, because more often than not, that weather will be heading your way. Of course, you can't just ignore the eastern half of the sky. It's entirely possible for a storm to blow in from any point on the compass. The best advice is, any time you see

A cloud that suddenly grows vertically can lead to trouble—like severe wind and lightning.

something approaching, from any direction, pay heed.

Clouds are usually the best visual indicators of what's coming. There are three basic cloud shapes: cumulus (puffy), stratus (spread out or layered), and nimbus (raining). Clouds appear at three altitudes: high (18,000 feet and above), medium-high (6,500 to 18,000 feet) and low (6,500 feet and below). Generally, high clouds indicate a weather change within the next twenty-four hours or so, while medium-high clouds tell you something's coming in the next six to twelve hours. By the time you see low nimbus clouds, you're already in the middle of what's happening.

More important than the clouds' shape and height, however, is their behavior. If those nice, puffy cumulus clouds suddenly begin to grow vertically, especially if they're over water, keep an eye on them and start making your way to a safe port. Generally speaking, when the clouds become taller than they are wide, trouble's brewing. This is classic thunderstorm behavior, especially on hot, humid days, and could indicate the leading edge of a cold front, meaning you could soon be in for severe winds and lightning. And if the height of the clouds seems to be dropping noticeably, an effect called a lowering ceiling, it usually means a warm front is imminent, along with potential storms.

Clouds aren't the only indicators of impending weather changes. Shifting winds usually mean something is afoot, especially winds shifting from the north to the west and then to the south (often a good indicator that rain's on the way). A sudden and dramatic increase or decrease in wind speed also means something's about to happen. And if you notice that not only has the wind really picked up, but that the temperature seems to have dropped, a situation sometimes called a "gust front," it's almost a sure sign that you're about to get hammered by a thunderstorm. What you're feeling is usually a burst of cool air flowing out of the base of a storm.

It's a good idea to have a barometer onboard and to check it every few hours. A barometer and a compass, so you know which way the wind's blowing, can tell you quite a bit about the weather in the immediate future. A falling barometer usually means bad weather is on the way, a steady barometer means no change, and rising barometric pressure indicates better things to come. (See table below for a fuller explanation of wind, pressure, and forecast.)

Wind	Barometric Pressure	Forecast
SW to NW	30.10 to 30.20 and steady	fair for the next 1–2 days
SW to NW	30.10 to 30.20 and rising rapidly	fair, followed by rain within 2 days
SW to NW	30.20 or above and steady	continued fair
SW to NW	30.20 or above and falling slowly	increasing temperature and fair for 2 days
S to SE	30.10 to 30.20 and falling slowly	rain within 24 hours
S to SE	30.10 to 30.20 and falling rapidly	increasing wind and rain within 12–24 hours
SE to NE	30.10 to 30.20 and falling slowly	rain within 12–18 hours
SE to NE	30.10 to 30.20 and falling rapidly	increasing wind and rain within 12 hours
E to NE	30.10 and above and falling slowly	in summer, fair; in winter, rain within 24 hours
E to NE	30.10 and above and falling rapidly	in summer, rain within 12–24 hours; in winter, increasing winds and rain or snow
SE to NE	30.00 or below and falling slowly	rain continuing 1–2 days
SE to NE	30.00 or below and falling rapidly	rain and high wind, clearing within 36 hours
S to SW	30.00 or below and rising slowly	clearing within a few hours, fair for several days
S to E	29.80 or below and falling rapidly	severe storm imminent, clearing within 24 hours
E to N	29.80 or below and falling rapidly	severe NE gale and heavy precipitation
Going to W	29.80 or below and rising rapidly	clearing

> **You may start out like Oscar Madison, but soon you'll be neater than Felix Unger.**

Even on a great day, it's important to maintain a more or less constant weather watch. Conditions can change quickly, especially in the spring and summer months. More than that, though, is the fact that reading the weather is a skill that has to be learned over time. At first, even if you're paying attention, many of the signs are so subtle as to seem unnoticeable. Before long, though, you'll find that you're not only seeing more signs, but that you're seeing them sooner. At the same time, you'll be building up a mental history not just of the signs you're seeing, but the events they forecast, making your readings more and more accurate and helpful.

Many of weather's side effects are obvious, but there's at least one side effect that may come as a surprise: your need for electricity onboard. In summer, especially in hot weather areas, you'll most likely need to run the air conditioner and a fan in the cabin to keep it tolerable. Without an air conditioner and fan, there's not nearly enough circulation below deck to keep things cool, even with the portholes wide open. In winter, especially up north, you'll need to run heaters to keep from freezing. Kent Doyle keeps six heaters going during the winter, including one that looks like a wood-burning stove, complete with a red lightbulb he calls the "flame" of his "almost fireplace." Donna Emmons uses space heaters too, but says her best defense against freezing New England winter nights is her electric mattress pad.

Summer or winter, it takes electricity to keep your boat's cabin comfortable. It takes electricity to keep the cabin functioning, too, from powering the refrigerator to recharging your computer and cell phone batteries. There are three ways to keep the juice flowing: shore power, electric generator, or the engine's alternator. (Sailors only get to choose from the first two options.) All three options provide constant electricity, and each works best in a specific situation. Shore power, obviously, is the way to go when you're at the marina. The electric generator is the choice when you're anchored or docked where shore power is not available (or if you're under sail). The engine's alternator will provide all the power you need when you're underway.

When you're not worrying about the weather or obsessing over electricity, you'll probably be tidying up. You may start your time living and working onboard as Oscar Madison, but within a few days, I guarantee you'll be such a neatnik that Felix Unger would look slovenly in comparison.

KEEP IT CLEAN

There's a reason why "shipshape" means neat and clean, and why career Navy men and women are the consummate neat freaks. When you're living in a closed environment, where every square inch of space is precious, you can't afford to be a slob. Clutter is the ultimate enemy, conspiring to trip you up at every step by having something sharp everywhere you try to sit, and hiding everything you might possibly need or want. Even something as innocuous as a small pile of dirty clothes has potential to impede onboard life.

It can become a huge issue if you're onboard with a partner and you have different tolerances for clutter and mess. Even on land, I'm the one who's constantly straightening up and Carey's the one complaining that the clothes I just put in the washer "weren't that dirty." In a house, where there's lots of room and plenty of opportunity to work around clutter,

This space contains your kitchen, living room, family room, office, and dining room. The smaller the boat, the harder it is to deal with piles of clutter.

Put cedar chips in cabinets, closets, and drawers to absorb odors and moisture.

it's no big deal. Onboard, with limited space and no escape from the mess, we knew we would have to work out a compromise.

DRAW SOME BOUNDARIES

The only way to keep the boat shipshape is to draw some boundaries before you ever move onboard. Determine between yourselves how the boat is going to be run. If dishes and silverware are to be washed and stowed after every meal, so be it, but that should be clarified beforehand. If it's okay to let the dirty clothes pile up in the closet until there's nothing clean onboard and you have to make a run to the laundromat, that's also an option. Eventually, everyone who makes a go of this figures out a way to deal with cleanliness. It's easier if you talk about it and try to work out a system before you move onboard. Just remember that living and working onboard is an evolutionary experience. Be sure to allow your system to change to suit your situation.

Part of the tidiness obsession comes from sheer necessity. With limited cupboard space, you won't be bringing a full china service along. Carey and I whittled our dishware/silverware down to two full sets: dinner plates, salad plates, soup bowls, knives, forks (not including salad forks), and spoons, two of each. With the two of us plus the dogs and cat onboard, we thought we'd never be inviting anyone over to dinner, so we only needed enough for ourselves. We also brought a skeleton crew of cooking utensils. We did bring extra coffee mugs and beer, wine, and cocktail glasses, because we could see having guests for drinks.

Kitchen Gear Checklist

► 6-quart stock pot with lid
► 4-quart stock pan with lid
► 2.5-quart stock pot with lid
► 10-inch frying pan
► Colander
► Whisk
► Large slotted spoon
► Ladle
► Spatula
► 8-inch butcher knife
► Bread knife
► Knife sharpener
► 8-inch tongs
► Cutting board
► Handheld grater
► Egg slicer
► Vegetable peeler
► Can opener
► Multipurpose corkscrew
► Large mixing bowl with lid
► Salad spinner
► Plastic storage bowls,
  various sizes

Tom MacNaughton gave me some excellent advice about cooking onboard. "Remember that meals onboard should get simpler and more

Keep rolls of quarters handy so you're always ready to use a laundromat.

robust," he said. "If you're inclined to say you're a gourmet cook, I would suggest you start thinking about all the gourmet food which is based upon robust dishes of ordinary people in various parts of the world. Stick to those." Then he added, "Always have the ingredients for chocolate brownies onboard. You can always make this into brownies, but we have found that you really need it when a storm has been blowing for a couple of days and you're very tired and perhaps have been seasick. At that point, you mix up a batch of brownie batter and just eat it raw. I don't know why this works, but it's a great restorative when you need it." Be sure, though, if you use raw eggs in your mix, to keep the batter refrigerated.

When it comes to clothing, even the most fastidious dressers find themselves wearing the same clothes for days on end. Unfortunately, living and working onboard means, obviously, that all your clothes and linens will, like you and your boat, be in close proximity to water at all times. And that proximity to water means mold and mildew, especially when it comes to swimsuits, shorts, and T-shirts.

Moldy and mildewed clothes bring up another reason tidiness becomes obsessive. Even if you spend every waking hour in the cockpit, you still find yourself sleeping in a confined area, which you do not want to share with moldy, mildewed clothes, or anyone wearing them.

Cedar chips, according to Dan Flatley, a friend based in Dallas, are the most important accessories in your onboard closets and drawers. Just toss the chips in the drawer beneath the clothes, and they will help absorb odors as well as moisture. The second-most-important nonclothing items—Dan and his wife, Sharon, swear—are rolls of quarters, so that you can hit every possible laundromat and wash every single of item of clothing you own, every chance you get.

One part of an onboard routine could be as simple—and crucial—as making sure the fresh water tanks are full enough for your next shower.

A PLACE FOR EVERYTHING

The most important aspect of keeping things shipshape and tidy, though, is to always know where things are. You only have so much space, so everything has to have more than one purpose. On land, you may have six corkscrews, fourteen ties, seven pairs of shoes, and so forth. Losing or misplacing anything isn't a big deal. Even a credit card or a driver's license can be replaced in a couple of days. But on the water, if you lose or misplace anything, you're in trouble, especially if you're 35 miles offshore.

It may be an offshoot of the need for tidiness, but everyone I've known who's spent extended time living and working onboard has become a creature of habit. Maybe routine gives a sense of security, maybe it just makes life onboard easier, or maybe it's a combination of both. Even though you may go into this with thoughts of a totally free and unencumbered lifestyle, before long you find yourself following a fairly strict routine without even realizing it. There are various and sundry things to take care of on a daily basis, even if you're using your boat as a floating apartment that never leaves the dock. Following a

No matter how pristine a lake may look, don't use its water for more than bathing without purifying it first.

> As a practical measure, liveaboards use the heads at marinas when they can.

routine helps make sure you never forget anything large or small.

Kent Bridges' lifestyle is a good example of how you can fall into a routine even if you don't have to. Since he pulled his Chris-Craft into the slip at Pete's Harbor, the boat's not been unmoored. His only real maintenance chores are making sure the fresh water tanks are full enough for his next shower, the purification system is working, and the sanitation system is emptying the gray water bilge when necessary. He also has to check that the shore power connection is secure. The whole procedure probably takes him five minutes. Yet you can almost set your watch by his daily routine, right down to the time he sits down for dinner at the marina restaurant and how many glasses of wine he has.

It's possible that living and working onboard appeals to a somewhat obsessive-compulsive personality type. In other words, the experience doesn't make you into a neat freak and a creature of habit, but rather, you had those tendencies anyway. Moving onboard just speeds up the process. Whatever the root cause, there are a number of systems and items that must be monitored and serviced daily or almost daily, even if you never leave the dock. If you go cruising over an extended time or distance, the number of systems and items you have to worry about increases. Routine helps you remember everything.

WATER, WATER…WHERE?

One of the benefits of a new boat like the Cobalt 360 is the reduced likelihood of something breaking down. Even on a brand-new boat, though, there are things you have to deal with that you never even think about when living the landlubbing life. For example, drinking water. At home, you turn on the tap and out it comes. In twenty-first century America, we take clean, abundant water for granted. Move onboard, though, and "water, water, everywhere, but not a drop to drink" suddenly rings true. On a freshwater lake, you can usually safely use unfiltered lake water for showers (be careful with kids, though, because they tend to swallow more water while bathing), and you might be able to use that same unfiltered lake water for washing dishes if you boil it first. You can also boil lake water and make it drinkable, but that's a huge hassle. In saltwater environments, of course, you can't bathe with or drink the water no matter what you do to it. You have to bring fresh water along.

Any boat suitable for living and working aboard will have a freshwater hold that you can refill with potable water at any marina. But even potable water can have microorganisms and bacteria that can breed in the hold. At the very least, you should invest in a product such as the Katadyn Micropur Forte Water Preservative, which prevents contamination from bacteria and algae. Unlike chlorine products, which are only active for a few hours, Micropur stays active up to six months and has a neutral taste. Of course, you have to be diligent about using it and remembering when it's time for a new treatment. Add one more item to your routine: for further purifying onboard freshwater, replace filters in the water filtration system regularly—every six to eight months, depending on use.

Even more important is regular treatment and maintenance of the waste system. Again, this is something most of us don't give a second thought to when on land. Use the facilities, flush, you're done. Arrange for a good cleaning of the systems on a regular basis and that's that. It's different onboard. When you're on land, whatever goes down the drain goes far enough away for you not to have to think about it until it's time, if you're on a septic system, to have the crew come out and handle the five-year maintenance. On a boat, you're essentially using a septic system with a very limited capacity that's only a few feet away from you at all times.

If you slack off treating and maintaining your waste system, you'll regret it. There are any number of head treatment products that work very well, controlling odors and keeping your system running at peak performance, but these products only work if you use them religiously. And even the best of them won't prevent you from having to remember to empty the bilge as often as possible to further control odors and keep things running smoothly.

If you're living and working in a small, closed space like a boat cabin, head odors are something you'll quickly learn to prevent, along with the smells of wet, mildewy clothes and dirty dishes left out overnight. That's why even the slobs among us quickly develop a routine that eliminates as

> ## TIP
> The bilge is a fine place to store heavy things like cans. However, bilge storage is rough on cans' paper labels, which tend to come off. Use a marker to identify the can's contents directly on the can itself, then discard the label before storage.

This galley looks spacious, but has limited counter and food-preparation space. Even on large boats, your galley area is likely to be smaller than a home kitchen.

many of these odors as possible. That is also why, whenever possible, liveaboards use the heads at marinas rather than on their boats.

Routine ensures that the little things are attended to without having to consult a daily to-do calendar. But for the first few days onboard, a daily to-do calendar is a must to help establish that routine and keep you from forgetting any of the little things. It's an especially good tool if you're an inexperienced boater, as some things are easily overlooked. This was our first to-do calendar:

Morning

▶ Start coffeemaker.

▶ Start computers; log on to *www.weather.gov* for severe weather alerts, then log on to *www.weather.com* to see hour-by-hour forecast for the day and animated radar.

▶ Check all lines for secure mooring, as well as for fraying and chafing. Make note to replace if necessary.

▶ Check shore power connection if docked.

▶ Treat freshwater hold/head if due.

▶ Fill freshwater hold if possible.

▶ Make bed, stow filler cushions if used.

- ▶ Start engine, check onboard systems, run bilge pump.
- ▶ Clean and stow coffeemaker after use.
- ▶ Go to work.

If Traveling

- ▶ Chart course.
- ▶ Check weather for duration of course and destination port (if one-way trip).
- ▶ Secure mooring at destination port before departing current port.
- ▶ Create and file float plan.
- ▶ If leaving for extended period, check P.O. box, pay any bills that will come due before anticipated return date.
- ▶ Allow sufficient travel time to ensure arrival at port well before sunset.
- ▶ Secure boat upon arrival. Set lines, attach shore power.

Evenings

- ▶ Check lines for secure mooring, check shore power for secure connection.
- ▶ Empty wastewater hold if possible.
- ▶ Check overnight weather forecasts and radar. Make preparations as needed.
- ▶ Clean and stow all dishes, flatware, cooking utensils, etc.

Food is different when you're living and working onboard. Even on a large boat, galleys and food storage areas are pretty small. The refrigerator is used for most of the onboard food storage because its low humidity keeps perishable and mold-susceptible items like bread fresh as long as possible. Canned goods are your best friends onboard, whether you're docked or cruising, and many stores will special-order canned goods for you. The Mealtime.org website (*www.mealtime.org*) is an invaluable resource for recipes based on easily obtained canned foods.

You can't talk about adjusting to life onboard without mentioning the dreaded specter of motion sickness. I've never suffered from it, but I'm one of the lucky ones. People who have gone their whole lives without having a problem with motion sickness can find themselves

Allow sufficient time to reach your port before sunset.

absolutely miserable after twenty-four hours onboard a gently but constantly rocking boat. Even a 50-foot yacht rocks and rolls almost constantly, even in smooth glassy water, whenever anyone moves about. And the smaller the boat, the more susceptible it is to motion.

Fortunately, the solution's pretty simple: Keep a large package of Dramamine onboard, and use it if you need to. Nobody's going to be impressed by the fact that you were sick for three days and didn't take the medicine that was in the cabinet. Going above deck to the cockpit where you can see the horizon is a time-tested stomach-calmer, as is ginger ale.

It may sound as if the moment you move onboard, you'll become a slave to routine and order, spending all your time obsessing over minutiae. But that won't happen. You will find yourself paying more attention to detail, but that's not such a bad thing. Before long it all becomes but a part of everyday life. You'll get in the habit of doing things regularly and taking care of things as they arise, and you'll spend more time doing what you came onboard to do in the first place—live, work, relax, and get a new perspective.

Tom MacNaughton told me a beautiful story about getting that new perspective. The MacNaughtons were in a Florida harbor when a fancy new yacht arrived and the owner came by for a visit. The owner, Tom remembers, "was faultlessly dressed in the red pants and polo shirt manner." He introduced himself and proceeded to describe the six-month dissolution of a retirement dream.

"It doesn't take very long to make a graceful, leisurely trip down the Intracoastal from the Chesapeake to Florida, but their refrigeration system kept breaking down. Week after week would find them stopped somewhere waiting for expensive parts, paying for the proper repair people to come help and so on. The refrigeration unit was ruining the retirement dream. He asked what kind of refrigeration unit we had. I said, 'We don't have any refrigeration system.'"

"With absolute incredulity, he said, 'You mean you use an icebox?!?'" Tom's boat was a British cruising yacht built in 1938. "It had never even had an icebox," Tom explains. "We kept our ginger beer in the bilge, which kept it cool enough for us. I believe the man actually started to become angry as I started to talk about buying canned meats and that wax-coated eggs would keep for weeks. Without a word in parting, he left."

"To me," Tom says, "the lesson to be learned here is not that you shouldn't have refrigeration, but that you shouldn't let refrigeration ruin your lifelong dream."

CHAPTER 6

SAFETY AND SEAMANSHIP

IF YOUR ENTIRE LIVING AND WORKING ONBOARD EXPERIENCE IS SPENT MOORED AT THE SAME SLIP AT THE SAME MARINA, SEAMANSHIP ISN'T AS CRUCIAL A COMPONENT TO YOUR SUCCESS AS IT IS IF YOU PLAN ON ACTUALLY GETTING OUT FROM TIME TO TIME. THE FACT THAT YOU'RE EVEN CONSIDERING LIVING AND WORKING ONBOARD A BOAT PROBABLY MEANS THAT YOU HAVE A BETTER THAN BASIC KNOWLEDGE OF SEAMANSHIP AND BOAT OPERATION, BUT EVEN IF YOU'RE A CRUSTY OLD SALT WHO'S SPENT MORE TIME ON WATER THAN ON LAND, YOUR PARTNER OR YOUR KIDS MIGHT NOT BE IN THE SAME, WELL, BOAT. AND ONE OF THE UNBREAKABLE RULES OF LIVING AND WORKING ONBOARD IS THAT EVERYONE WHO SPENDS TIME ON A BOAT MUST KNOW BASIC SEAMANSHIP. EVERYONE SHOULD KNOW HOW TO OPERATE THE BOAT, HOW TO TIE BASIC KNOTS, AND HOW TO PERFORM BASIC EMERGENCY PROCEDURES.

CONTENTS

- ▶ Float Plans
- ▶ Being Prepared
- ▶ Signs and Markers
- ▶ Shallows and Tides
- ▶ Anchoring
- ▶ Insurance

If you take your boat out of the marina at all, you must know basic seamanship and safety procedures.

Leaving basic boat handling skills aside for a moment, the number-one rule is that any time you leave port, you file a float plan, even if you're only going out for the day to check out a new waterside restaurant across the lake. A float plan ensures that someone on shore knows your starting point, your intended destination, and the course you plan to follow. This way, if something happens and you don't show up, time and energy will not be wasted by your potential rescuers.

FLOAT PLANS: YOUR EXTRA INSURANCE POLICY

Filing a float plan is simple. All you do is appoint an onshore contact and give them your plans for the day. This can be done over the phone, via e-mail, or fax. You also arrange a specific time window to get in touch with your contact and let them know you've arrived safely for the night.

Your float plan can be as detailed or as general as you want, the rule of thumb being that the plan's specificity should reflect your own. If you're going out to goof off for the day, your float plan may be as simple as "9:00 a.m.—Leave Lakeway Marina. Spend day on Lake Travis. 7:00 p.m.—Return to Lakeway Marina." If you're going to be working your way up the Intracoastal from Miami to Savannah, with lots of stops, your float plan will obviously be much more detailed.

Here's an example of a float plan that can be downloaded from the U.S. Coast Guard's website (*www.uscgboating.org*):

1. **Person Reporting Overdue Boat**

    Name _____ Phone _____

    Address _____

2. **Description of Boat**

    Name _____

    Registration/Documentation No. _____ Length _____

    Make _____ Type _____

    Hull Color _____ Trim Color_____

    Fuel Capacity _____ Engine Type _____ No. of Engines _____

    Distinguishing Features _____

    _____

3. **Operator of Boat**

   Name _____

   Age _____

   Health _____ Phone _____

   Address _____

   _____

   Operator's Experience _____

   _____

   _____

4. **Survival Equipment (Check as Appropriate)**

   ❏ #___PFDs   ❏ Flares   ❏ Mirror

   ❏ Smoke Signals   ❏ Flashlight   ❏ Food

   ❏ Paddles   ❏ Water   ❏ Anchor

   ❏ Raft or Dinghy   ❏ EPIRB   ❏ Others

5. **Marine Radio: ❏ Yes ❏ No**

   Type _____ Freqs. _____

   Digital Selective Calling (DSC) ❏ Yes ❏ No

6. **Trip Expectations**

   Depart from _____

   Departure Date _____ Time _____

   Going to _____

   Arrival Date _____ Time _____

   If operator has not arrived/returned by:

   Date_____Time _____

   call the Coast Guard or local authority at the following number:

   _____

   _____

7. **Vehicle Description**

   License No. _____ Make _____

   Model _____ Color _____

   Where is vehicle parked? _____

   _____

   _____

> **TIP**
>
> The US. Coast Guard's website offers valuable information about preventing injuries and staying safe.

PFDs for Adults

Personal Flotation Devices (PFDs) aren't just a good idea. They're the law. Federal safety requirements state that there must be one PFD for each person onboard, plus one Type IV (throwable PFD). PFD design has come a long way in the past few decades: there are models made with all kinds of boaters and conditions in mind. Here are a few:

A vest designed for ease of motion for active boaters.

A vest designed for use on sailboats.

This "bomber-style" PFD combines flotation with foul-weather protection.

8. Persons Onboard

Name	Age	Phone	Medical Conditions

9. Additional Information

Complete this form before you set out and leave it with (or e-mail or fax it to) a reliable person who can be depended upon to notify the Coast Guard or other rescue organization should you not return as scheduled. Do not file this plan with the Coast Guard. Remember to contact your friend in case of delay and upon your return.

Don't specify an exact time for contact upon arrival, such as 5:30 p.m., because time has a way of getting away from you when you're out on the water having fun. The better idea is to tell your onshore contact you'll call them, for example, between 7:00 p.m. and 9:00 p.m. If you haven't called by 9:00 p.m., your onshore contact will try to get in touch with you, just in case you've forgotten to call (it happens) or have been delayed.

If your contact can't reach you within thirty minutes, he or she should then alert the authorities, using the float plan to pinpoint, as closely as possible, your estimated location.

In addition to filing float plans, you need to make sure you're prepared for an emergency. The vast majority of boaters never have to deal with anything more momentous than running out of gas or getting stuck on a sand bar, and that's the way we all like it. Still, something catastrophic could happen, and we must be ready.

EMERGENCY KIT

Assembling an emergency kit and knowing how to use everything in it is the first step in dealing with an unexpected and unpleasant situation. There must be a personal flotation device (PFD) for each person onboard. (That's not just a rule of thumb; it's the rule of law.) In addition to PFDs, your emergency preparedness kit should include a VHF (very high frequency) radio, a GPS (global positioning system) unit so you can fix and broadcast your position to help rescuers find you, a fire extinguisher (or two), a first-aid kit, and, if you're going offshore, a flare gun and/or an EPIRB (Electronic Position Indicating Radio Beacon) or GPIRB (Global Position Indicating Radio Beacon). If you're going to be out of sight of land, the last two items have been called the "best life insurance policy you can buy." Of the two, the GPIRB is preferred, because its built-in GPS allows the unit to pinpoint your position more precisely and much more quickly than the EPIRB. GPIRBs aren't cheap—prices start at around $1,500 per unit—but they're worth it. In an offshore emergency, the GPIRB unit uses its GPS to fix your position and then broadcasts that position as well as a distress signal that rescuers can use to find you. Once activated, the GPIRB will broadcast your updated position—in case you're drifting—every twenty minutes.

WHAT TO DO WHEN SOMETHING BAD HAPPENS

The majority of emergencies fall into three broad categories: boat damage (including leaks, swamping, and capsizing), fires or explosions, and medical emergencies. Regardless of which category an emergency falls into, the immediate response is always the same: Put on PFDs. Drowning is the number-one cause of death on the water, and it's almost always preventable by simply donning a life jacket.

Dealing with damage to the boat is relatively straightforward. Determine the extent of the damage, repair if possible, and head for safety. If the boat is taking on water or becoming swamped, start the

PFDs for Kids

A children's vest—note the handle extending from the back, which is to aid an adult in hauling a child from the water if necessary.

Your onboard safety kit should help you stay out of trouble as well as assist you in getting help when trouble can't be averted. Items in the kit should include:

- A handheld GPS unit to provide detailed barometric, compass, and map data.
- A pair of fire extinguishers—two so you have a backup if one fails.
- Flares. New ones can be safely hand-fired, no longer requiring launching from guns.
- GPIRB unit—the best investment you hope you'll never use. If needed, it will send a GPS-tagged distress signal, bringing help straight to you.

bilge pump and, if necessary, start bailing. Don't cut the motor unless the leak is coming from the engine's hoses. If the situation deteriorates, send a distress signal and stay with the boat if possible.

Fires and explosions are deadly, because you can't escape the area. Use the FIRE (find, inform, restrict, extinguish) procedures to deal with the situation. First, find the fire and determine its size. Inform by sounding an alarm (if there are other people onboard), then make a distress call to the Coast Guard and other vessels and activate fire-fighting equipment. Restrict the fire by closing hatches and ports to shut off its air supply, cutting off electric power to the affected area, setting up boundaries to contain the fire, and cutting off the fire's fuel and ventilation, and then maneuver the boat to minimize the wind's effect on the fire. Extinguish the fire using appropriate materials and establish a reflash watch to make sure it doesn't flare back up. Finally, count heads to make sure everyone's still onboard and okay. If the fire can't be brought under control, prepare to abandon ship. This is a last resort and, if taken, should be broadcast with your distress signal.

Medical emergencies may be the scariest of all because the panic potential is so great. This is where taking a Red Cross CPR class can make all the difference, whether you're confronted with the emergency while out on the water or moored at the marina. Stabilize the injured person(s) as well as you can and begin first-aid procedures. Don't attempt any procedures you don't know. If all you know how to do is apply a Band-Aid, then that's all you can do. In these situations, it's better to do nothing than to do the wrong thing. If you're under way, once the injured person is onboard and stabilized, send a distress call that indicates your heading so rescuers can either intercept you en route to shore or at least be standing by when you arrive. Don't rush to shore. The bouncing and jarring of a high-speed ride can make things much worse. Simply head for shore as directly and smoothly as possible while sending distress signals updating your position, heading, and the injured person's status. If the injured person is in the water, do not try to lift him or her aboard unless it's absolutely unavoidable. It's much safer to get a PFD or life ring to the person and wait for help to arrive.

DON'T LEAVE THE DOCK WITHOUT IT

Along with preparing an emergency kit and reacquainting yourself (and anybody else onboard) with basic emergency procedures, before setting out you should refer to the Coast Guard's predeparture checklist to make sure you haven't forgotten anything. It's available online at the Coast Guard's website, as well as here:

Boater's Predeparture Checklist

Know your vessel. Before departure, always be sure your vessel is in good working condition and properly equipped for emergencies. Avoid inconvenience and potential danger by taking a few minutes to check the following:

Minimum Federal Required Equipment	Yes	No
State Registration Documentation	❏	❏
State Numbering Displayed	❏	❏
Certificate of Documentation	❏	❏
Life jackets (PFDs)—one for each person	❏	❏
Throwable PFD	❏	❏
Visual Distress Signals	❏	❏
Fire Extinguishers (fully charged)	❏	❏
Proper Ventilation	❏	❏
Backfire Flame Arrestor	❏	❏
Sound Producing Device(s)	❏	❏
Navigation Lights	❏	❏
Oil Pollution Placard	❏	❏
Garbage Placard	❏	❏
Marine Sanitation Device	❏	❏
Navigation Rules	❏	❏
Any Additional State Requirements	❏	❏

Besides meeting the federal requirements, prudent boaters carry auxiliary safety equipment. The following additional items are suggested depending on the size, location, and use of your boat:

Recommended Equipment	Yes	No	N/A
VHF Marine Radio	❏	❏	❏
Anchor and Tackle	❏	❏	❏

Preventing fires from getting started in the first place is the best defense.

Chart(s) of Area & Navigation Tools	❏	❏	❏
Magnetic Compass	❏	❏	❏
Fenders and Boat Hook	❏	❏	❏
Mooring Lines and Heaving Line	❏	❏	❏
Manual Bilge Pump or Bailing Device	❏	❏	❏
Tool Kit	❏	❏	❏
Spare Parts (fuses, spark plugs, belts, etc.)	❏	❏	❏
Spare Battery (fully charged)	❏	❏	❏
Spare Propeller	❏	❏	❏
Extra Fuel & Oil	❏	❏	❏
Alternate Propulsion (paddles/oars)	❏	❏	❏
Flashlight & Batteries	❏	❏	❏
Search Light	❏	❏	❏
First-Aid Kit	❏	❏	❏
Sunscreen (SPF 30+)	❏	❏	❏
Mirror	❏	❏	❏
Food and Water	❏	❏	❏
Extra Clothing	❏	❏	❏
AM / FM Radio	❏	❏	❏
Cellular Phone	❏	❏	❏

	Yes	No	N/A
Binoculars	❏	❏	❏
Safety Checks and Tests	Yes	No	N/A
Test marine radio (voice call)	❏	❏	❏
Test navigation and anchor lights	❏	❏	❏
Test steering (free movement)	❏	❏	❏
Test tilt / trim	❏	❏	❏
Test bilge pump	❏	❏	❏
Check for any excessive water in bilges	❏	❏	❏
Check fuel system for any leaks	❏	❏	❏
Check engine fluids	❏	❏	❏
Ensure boat plug is properly installed	❏	❏	❏
Check electrical system	❏	❏	❏
Check galley / heating systems	❏	❏	❏
Check gauges (i.e., batteries)	❏	❏	❏
Check fuel amount	❏	❏	❏
Ensure anchor is ready for use	❏	❏	❏
Check load of vessel & secure gear from shifting	❏	❏	❏
Verify that passengers know emergency procedures and equipment location	❏	❏	❏
Everyone put on life jackets to check for proper fitting	❏	❏	❏
Check the weather forecast	❏	❏	❏
File a float plan with family or friend	❏	❏	❏

FEELING THE DRAFT

Even with float plans filed and appropriate safety equipment onboard, boaters can get themselves into real trouble if they overlook the obvious when cruising or exploring—for instance, the size and draft of their boat. Oddly enough, this is often a bigger problem in familiar waters than around a strange port. Many boaters have grown up on smaller boat, ski boats, and runabouts, so they have a good idea where they can safely take those boats on waters they know. But when they make the move to living and working onboard, they usually step up dramatically in size and draft, so waters they could easily navigate in a 20-foot runabout are now treacherously shallow.

Little draft (left).
Lots of draft (right).

Before deciding to have a go at living and working onboard, I spent a lot of time on Lake Austin on a MasterCraft X30 wakeboard boat. The X30 has an LOA of 22'8" and a draft of 22.5". The Cobalt 360, with an LOA of 36' and a draft of 42" (drive down) was an increase of 14 feet in length and almost double the amount of draft. If I had started running on instinct and hit some of my traditional coves, I would have run the Cobalt aground in a New York minute.

This is why it's important to have charts onboard and to use them. You'll at least have an idea of water depth and submerged obstacles, as well as a depth meter with an alarm you can set for 12- to 18-inches deeper than your boat's draft (on the Cobalt, I set the alarm for 5.5', giving myself a full 24-inch margin of error). It's also a good idea, especially in coastal areas, to make sure you have tide charts so you'll be able to factor the tide into the equation. If the tide's a big one and it's going out fast, you might want to know that so you can head for deeper, safer water while there's still time.

SIGNS AND MARKERS

Knowing where you're going and how to get from Point A to Point B safely is important away from tides and the coast, too. In fact, unless you're on a private ski lake, you absolutely need to know basic navigation. Luckily, these basics are easy to come by.

The first thing to do is check out the U.S. Coast Guard's website, where you can find the "rules of the road" (*www.navcen.uscg.gov/mwv/navrules/rotr_online.htm*). You don't have to memorize every one of these rules, but you do need to be familiar with most of them. Most of us can't recite our local automotive laws, either, but we have a pretty good idea of what they involve. The rules of the waterway should be the same.

Following the rules of the road in a car is made easier by all the roadway signs. Speed limits, yield and stop signs, traffic lights, and dozens of other markers tell you what to expect and what you're supposed to be doing. The waterways are filled with similar signs and markers. You just have to learn what they mean.

The primary aids to navigation are the channel markers. It's quite important to know that these usually mark the SIDES of the channels, not their center, so it does matter which side of the marker you pass on. Channel markers are generally either red or green, although there are some markers that are both red and green, and some markers that have yellow squares or triangles. Channel markers may also have flashing lights for better visibility at night or in fog, and some have horns.

Virtually all U.S. waterways follow the traditional rule: "Red, Right, Returning." This means that when returning from sea, you should keep the red markers on your right (or starboard) and the green markers on your left (port) in order to stay within the channel. The Intracoastal Waterway, which runs between Texas and New Jersey, has a special rule, in which a boat is considered to be returning from sea (hence keeping the red markers on the starboard side) when traveling in a generally southward direction.

Channel markers are also differentiated by shape

Cormorants perch on a red channel marker near the Chesapeake Bay. When returning from sea, keep red markers on your right.

and numbering. Red markers are triangular, while green markers are square. For example, red "nun" buoys have pointed peaks, while green "can" buoys are squared-off at the top, like a drum. Red markers are even-numbered, and green markers get the odds. The numbers also indicate whether you're heading toward shore or out to sea. The marker farthest out to sea will be #1, so as you approach shore the numbers get higher.

In a narrow-channel lake such as Lake Travis, knowing red from green is enough, but larger, multichannel lakes require a bit more knowledge, as do coastal areas.

FORK IN THE WATERWAY

Whenever a channel splits into two branches (bifurcates), a preferred-channel marker is used. These markers have red and green bands. To stay in the preferred or main channel, treat the marker as though it were only the color of the top band. (The shape of the buoy and the light, if the marker has one, will also indicate the dominant color.) So if you're heading toward shore and see a marker with a red band atop a green band, treat it as you would any red channel marker: keep it to the starboard side. Conversely, if the top band is green, keep the marker to port.

The Intracoastal Waterway (ICW) has special markers that come into play at the places when the ICW meets up with other waterways. In those places, buoys not only carry the traditional red or green colors but also have a yellow triangle or square. For those traveling the ICW, the yellow marking supersedes the red or green, with the yellow triangle representing a nun buoy, which is usually red, and a yellow square representing a can buoy, which is usually green.

It sounds confusing, but it's really not that bad. Any time you're using the ICW, simply follow the yellow markers, remembering that the triangles will always be on the shoreside of the channel, while the squares will always be on the seaside. So if you're traveling generally north on the ICW, keep the yellow squares to starboard and the yellow triangles to port. If you're heading generally south, keep the triangles to starboard and the squares to port.

If you're entering the ICW, the yellow markers will help you to go in the right direction. If you're returning from sea and want to go north on the ICW, follow your channel until you see a buoy with a yellow square. As you pass that buoy, turn to starboard and you'll have the correct heading. If you're coming in from the sea and want to go south on the ICW, stay in your channel until you see a buoy with a yellow triangle. Before you reach that buoy, turn to port (left), keeping the yellow triangle to starboard at all times. If you're heading out to sea, the opposite holds true.

The one other channel marker you may encounter is a mid-channel or "safe water" mark, sometimes referred to as a "welcome home" buoy because it's usually the first marker you encounter when returning from sea. This is a red and white buoy that sits, as the name implies, in the middle of the channel. If lighted, this buoy has a white light and will flash the Morse Code Alpha sequence (the letter A, represented by a short light followed by a long light, or "dot-dash"). There is safe passage on either side of a mid-channel marker.

Of course, finding that first mid-channel marker can be more difficult if you don't have charts onboard and a basic knowledge of how to read them. One of Carey's and my hard and fast rules is that we never leave the dock without charts covering every bit of water we may use that day, even if we're only cruising the length of Lake Travis. Charts let you know where you are and how to get where you're going safely.

For coastal boaters, channel markers and charts are as important as the paved parts of the highway and road maps are to drivers. For those of us who cruise inland, like Carey and me, the channel markers aren't usually so much aids to navigation as aids in avoiding running aground, since the channel markers show us where the safe, deep water is. Lake Travis is not a constant-level lake. During droughts the lake level can drop forty feet or more, making what was once a deep-water cove a shallow wading pool and exposing us to dangerous sand bars. So for safety's sake, we always stay in the channel when we're running on plane, and we use the charts to stay alert to potential submerged hazards.

> "For coastal boaters, channel markers and charts are as important as road maps are to drivers!"

Go slow when navigating shallows.
Trim the drive as much as possible.

NAVIGATING SHALLOWS

What should you do if for some reason you do find yourself in shallow waters? First, slow down. There are people who'll tell you that the smartest thing to do if you find yourself in shallow water is to stay on the throttle and stay on plane, figuring that on plane a boat only needs a few inches of water to stay afloat. Those people are wrong. Think of it this way: If you do run aground, do you want to do it at 45 mph or at idle?

Next, back off the throttle quickly, smoothly and gently, and then proceed at idle speed. This allows the depth finder to work more accurately so you can react to its readings more quickly, and if you do run aground, hull or outdrive damage will be kept to a minimum. If none of that matters, just remember that if you and your boat survive a high-speed grounding, it's a sure thing that you'll have to suffer the indignity of calling for help in getting your boat free and back under way, as well as quite probably wrecking all kinds of havoc on your stowed office equipment, even if it's been well-secured.

Trim up. The propellers and lower units are the components most vulnerable to damage in shallow water, so do what you can to protect them. In addition to slowing down, trim the drive up as much as possible while still getting propulsion. This raises the prop and outdrive to reduce the boat's draft (the Cobalt's draft, for example, reduces all the way to 27" with the drives up) and lessens the potential angle of impact if you do hit bottom. To see how this works, try this: make a fist with your left hand, representing the bottom or a submerged obstacle, and hold it up in front of your face. Hold your right hand open and perpendicular to the ground, representing your outdrive trimmed level. If you push your right hand into your left fist, you can see how the damage occurs. Now hold your right hand at a 45-degree angle to the ground, representing the drives trimmed up. You should be able to see immediately how the potential for damage is lessened.

> If you do run aground, do you want to do it at 45 mph or at idle?

TIP

Tides during full and new Moons are usually higher and lower than those during the first and last quarters.

TIDES

Although the tides don't affect those living and working onboard on lakes (except the Great Lakes) and rivers, they deserve a mention. If you have a lot of coastal and therefore tidal experience, you most likely know how to deal with the ebbs and flows, but problems can occur for inlanders who go coastal.

Keep in mind that as the moon orbits the earth, the tides move across the earth's surface. It takes the moon twenty-four hours and fifty minutes to orbit the earth, so the tides can be predicted with great accuracy well into the future. That's why tide tables for any location are so readily available at marinas, in newspapers, and online.

A tide table lets you know when the high and low tides will occur, as well as how high or low the tide will be. Tidal height isn't a constant. The moon's gravitational effect varies. It's strongest when the moon is full and new, and weakest at the first and last quarter. So the tides during the full and new moons, called spring tides, are usually higher and lower than those during the first and last quarter, called neap tides. This is important to know because in some situations, a high spring tide could be several meters higher (and a low tide several meters lower) than a corresponding neap tide.

Just like tidal height, tidal flow, in both spring and neap tides, isn't constant. The tide flows relatively slowly during the hour immediately preceding and following the high and low tide; the tidal flow is fastest in the hours immediately preceding and following the halfway point between high and low tide.

People who don't deal with tides regularly tend to forget that tides move vertically. As the water level rises, the waterline on shore will move horizontally due to the slope of the shoreline. The steeper the shoreline, the lesser the horizontal movement; the more level the shoreline, the greater the horizontal movement. This is important if you choose to spend the night at anchor, because you have to make sure that when the tide goes out, your boat won't be left high and dry on a sand bar.

ANCHORING TIPS

If you'll be spending the night at anchor instead of moored at a dock, the first thing to do is consult the tide table and nautical chart to make sure you're in water that's deep enough to navigate at low tide. Then figure out where the tide is when you're setting the anchor. If you're anchoring at low tide and the tide will rise by five feet, for example, you have to add six times that length to your rode (the anchor line), or 30 feet. If you forget to bring your tide table, you'll generally be safe if you figure your rode as you would for a nontidal area, then add about 40 feet, enough to allow for up to a six-foot tide. This isn't surefire, though, because there are places where the tide rises and falls as much as 14 feet, so remember that tide table when you set out.

If you do spend the night at anchor, whether it's in coastal waters or on an inland lake or river, be sure and do so safely so you can spend the night working or watching the stars or whatever it is you'd rather do than constantly mess with the anchor lines. Simple anchoring requires some room for the boat to swing around, so make sure you're in a wide-open area. If there are other boats around, ask them how much scope (scope is the ratio of anchor-line length to water depth; for overnight, a scope of six to one or greater is recommended—multiply the water's depth by six or more to calculate the proper line length) they're using so you can be sure to anchor far enough away to avoid bumping into one another. If you're the only boat in the area, make sure you anchor far enough away from shore or obstacles.

Measure the anchor line before dropping anchor, and secure the line to the bow cleat at that length. Point the bow into the wind or current (if there is any), stop the boat, and lower the anchor. As you lower the anchor, put the throttle in reverse and idle back to keep the anchor chain from getting in the way of the anchor digging into the bottom. When the line's completely out, keep idling back and watch the anchor line to see when the anchor sets. If the anchor is bouncing along the bottom, the line will bounce and jerk, too. When the anchor sets, the line will go taut and hold steady. Then it's time to find a reference point on shore that you can check to make sure you don't start drifting. (Anchors can work themselves loose, especially if the wind changes direction.)

ANCHOR LIGHTS

Even though you're not going anywhere, you need to use an anchor light to let other boaters know where you are and that you're not moving. An anchor light is a single, all-around white light mounted at the highest point on the boat, where it can best be seen by other boaters. Unless you're in an area where boat traffic can be expected—and you shouldn't be—you're not legally required to run anchor lights, but you should, at least until you're ready to turn in for the night.

Before you turn in, though, check the anchor line to make sure the anchor hasn't come loose. If it has, reset the anchor.

Anchor lights are mounted on the highest point on the boat.

INSURANCE

Finally, even if you've taken all safety precautions, brushed up on all your navigation and chart-reading skills, and know your boat's size and draft inside and out, you can still have an accident that causes costly damage to your boat. That's why not carrying insurance on your boat would be the height of recklessness.

There are a number of insurers that will write policies for boats and boaters. Based on positive experiences over the years, our choice is, was, and will be to carry insurance from BoatU.S. (*www.boatus.com*). Most people I know choose one of BoatU.S.'s major insurance programs, either the Total Protection Yacht Policy or the Basic Protection Boat Saver Policy. The Basic Protection Boat Saver Policy is more affordable, but since it's only available for boats 26 feet or less, it's not applicable to most of those who live and work onboard.

You wouldn't think of not insuring your home. Your boat needs protection against everything from hit-and-run boaters to hurricanes such as 1985's Gloria, responsible for the damage below.

The boat above flipped when the trailer fishtailed at a curve and the driver lost control of the car. Improper weight distribution was the cause of the mishap, but fishtailing can also occur when tires are too soft.

The Total Protection Yacht Policy is the best choice for most liveaboards, since it fully covers your boat against everything not specifically excluded. (Exclusions may vary.) The policy includes 24-hour emergency dispatch, $500,000 in fuel spill liability coverage including accidental or unintentional discharge of oil or fuel, a lifetime guarantee on repairs made at a BoatU.S.-approved facility (as long as you own the boat and are insured through BoatU.S.), investigative services to help settle warranty disputes or determine potential manufacturer's defects, full salvage assistance up to the value of your boat with no deductible, and uninsured boater protection so you're covered if involved in an accident with an uninsured boater or in a hit-and-run.

These are all important benefits of insurance, especially the uninsured boater and fuel spill liability. Although most lenders will require boat buyers to carry insurance as protection against the loss of the boat as collateral, there are no state or federal laws that require boaters to carry insurance. Many recreational boaters don't even carry a liability policy, which means that all too often, boating accidents will cause both parties to suffer substantial financial losses. It also means that hit-and-run accidents often go unpunished, as the guilty parties apparently decide it's cheaper to run away than take responsibility for their actions. Uninsured boater coverage, then, is something Carey and I decided we couldn't afford to be without.

COSTLY CLEANUP

Fuel spill liability is another issue that many boaters overlook to their lasting regret. If your boat spills fuel or oil, even as the result of sinking or an accident, federal and state laws can hold you liable for the costs of containment, cleanup, and environmental damage. A sinking, or any accident severe enough for your boat to discharge your supplies of fuel and oil, is devastating enough without facing a bill from the government for cleaning up your mess. Coverage is worth every penny.

Since we were staying in Lake Travis, we didn't have to worry about cruising extensions on our insurance policy, but BoatU.S. does offer such extensions for those venturing to Canada, the Bahamas, Bermuda, and Mexico. BoatU.S. also offers discounts for completing boater safety courses, so by becoming a better, safer boater, you save a few bucks.

Trailer Safety

To quote BoatU.S.'s *Seaworthy* magazine, "Boats not only go aground on the water. They can go aground on a highway."

Neglecting tires is one of the most frequent causes of trailer-related accidents. BoatU.S. cautions that the trailer tires sometimes need replacing long before treads wear out. Spiderweb cracks in the sidewall indicate that the tire is rotten and can no longer carry heavy weights.

Trailer tires can also suffer from underinflation. They should be checked before every trailer use. Look at the sidewalls for recommended inflation pressures.

A family thanks a Sea Tow skipper
for bringing them back to shore.

MARINE ASSISTANCE COVERAGE

Another type of coverage that's highly recommended is a towing "service contract." BoatU.S., under the name TowBoatU.S., and Sea Tow (*www.seatow.com*) are the two best-known purveyors of this service. Even if you're not going to live onboard, the coverage is worth the investment. Both Sea Tow and TowBoatU.S. offer free on-water towing, free soft ungroundings (if you've impaled your boat on a reef, however, that's a hard grounding and doesn't qualify), free battery jumps, and free fuel drops (boaters pay for the fuel, but not the drop). At some point in my boating life, I've found myself in need of every one of those services.

Even if the situation is not life-threatening but just a nuisance, the membership is a wallet saver. Commercial towing services charges $200 or more to motor out and bring you in. They start charging the minute they leave the dock, and the charges continue until the tow boat has returned to its own dock—NOT just until your boat has been safely delivered. Since many commercial services charge a one-hour minimum, a single towing can easily cost you more than the $119 annual membership fee Sea Tow currently charges.

CHAPTER 7

SPECIAL CHALLENGES

LIVING AND WORKING ONBOARD A BOAT MAY SEEM LIKE THE SORT OF BARE-BONES EXISTENCE THAT WOULD ALLOW YOU TO SAVE TONS OF MONEY, SO THAT WHEN YOU MOVED BACK ON LAND YOU'D BE ABLE TO BUY A PALACE AND LIVE IN THE ROYAL MANNER TO WHICH YOU'D LIKE TO BECOME ACCUSTOMED. IF ONLY THAT WERE THE CASE. THE REALITY OF THE SITUATION FOR MOST OF US IS THAT THIS LIFESTYLE CAN BE A VERY EXPENSIVE PROPOSITION.

Start with the boat itself. A new boat large enough for even one person to live and work aboard will cost at least $100,000. A used boat can be had for less, but may require more of an investment in repairs and upkeep. Then there are docking and slip fees. Any new equipment, from computers to TVs, will also add to your expenses. And those are just the obvious costs. Many others can sneak up on you.

CONTENTS

▶ Money Matters

▶ Food for Thought

▶ Isolation Chamber

▶ Staying in Shape

Many exercise options are available to liveaboards—
and only a few require going ashore.

The mid-berth area on the Cobalt 360 is only inches away from the galley—which makes washing the dishes before bedtime a necessity.

If you're an occasional boater, you may not notice how everything costs just a little bit more when you're closer to the water. If you're paying $1.50 per gallon for regular unleaded gas at the Texaco down the street, you can almost guarantee that you'll be paying $2.50 to $3.00 per gallon at the marina's gas docks.

Even postage and shipping must be considered. Postage is a cost that most people never consider when they think about living and working onboard. True, it costs exactly the same amount to mail a letter from a marina's post box as it does from the main post office downtown, but you also need mail delivered. You may have to get a P.O. box, because some marinas have postal service, some don't. If you want important papers such as paychecks delivered to the marina office, much less all the way to your transom, you may have to have them delivered via FedEx or

UPS, and more often than not, you'll have to pick up the cost. It's not cheap, but it can be convenient; if you're on a cruise and you know where you'll be docked the next morning, you can have FedEx or UPS deliver to that marina. Just contact the marina in advance and let them know you'll be expecting the delivery. Make sure the senders use the proper address instead of reentering the address of a marina where you docked last week.

YOUR DAILY BREAD

As expensive as FedEx, UPS and renting P.O. boxes may be, the costs are nothing compared to food. And while you can, theoretically, live without mail service, you won't make it very long without something to eat. Because onboard storage space is limited, you'll probably have to shop more frequently than you're used to.

Frequent grocery runs won't be the only adjustment your galley will require of you. If your boat is under 40 feet, your galley is likely to be a small open corner of your main living space, and you'll need to be prepared to clean it thoroughly, from counters and cutting boards to dishes and flatware, before going to bed every night. "Leave it for the morning" becomes a much less viable option when your sinkful of dirty dishes is just a few feet from your pillow.

And inevitably, there will be times when, after a long day on the water or a grueling day at work, the last thing you'll want to do as the sun sets is to start the cooking-and-cleaning cycle anew. "That's

Eating in a marina's restaurant provides a welcome opportunity to socialize with other liveaboards, but costs can quickly add up.

> **A gas grill that can be mounted on the cockpit's gunwales can save cleanup time and money.**

exactly how I see it," explains Kent Bridges. "It's a pain to have to cook for one, anyway. So I eat every meal at the Waterfront Restaurant at Pete's Harbor. It's just easier." Easier, but more expensive. Having Papa John's deliver a pizza or taking a sunset cruise to a favorite waterfront restaurant are always options, too. But these options can drive costs up quickly.

You can alleviate some of the money and cleanup problems by investing in a dockside gas grill that can be mounted on the cockpit's gunwales. These new barbecues use propane instead of charcoal, so they're safer and more environmentally friendly. Believe it or not, even the folks at Weber, probably the best-known of grill manufacturers, say that blind taste tests show that virtually no one can taste the difference between something grilled over charcoal or over gas. Charcoal does have a certain primal allure, and both art and science go into building and maintaining the perfect cooking fire. But out on the water, the ability to press a button and start cooking can't be overestimated, nor can the ease of cleanup without still-smoldering briquettes.

The grill makes cooking onboard more enjoyable because you're not cooped up below deck. It gives you the opportunity to save at least a little grocery money by either catching your own dinner, if you're an angler, or taking advantage of the ultrafresh and lower-cost catches that can often be purchased directly from the boats in coastal ports.

TALK ISN'T CHEAP

One potential source of surprise costs may be cellular telephone service. Depending on your business and personal calling habits, you may need a plan that offers long-distance calling at a single blanket rate. If you're going to move your boat around much, you'll do well to consider a plan that lets you avoid roaming charges. You may also want a multiphone "family plan" if you're not living alone. While all these options are readily available almost everywhere for prices that have dropped steadily of late, they still aren't as cheap as a land-based plan. As of this writing, getting all the options listed above may cost as much as $200 each month.

Entertainment can have its costs and inconveniences, too. Movie buffs should be prepared for the challenge of picking up and returning tapes and DVDs, especially if they intend to cruise up and down the coast rather than staying close to an inland marina. But the biggest entertainment bargain around is the XM or Sirius satellite radio, which runs about ten dollars per month and, for us, got more use than anything on the boat, including computers and telephones.

Not all onboard entertainment costs money, though. You can, as we did, anchor in a secluded cove on a hot August night, stretch out on the foredeck and fall asleep watching the Perseid meteor shower. You can watch the sun rise over water that appears to be steaming in the cool of a fall morning. In warm-water ports, you can go swimming any time you want. And you get to enjoy the unmitigated envy of all your friends who think that living and working onboard is the equivalent of discovering you have superpowers. Not many things are more entertaining than that.

But free meteor showers and the envy of your landlubbing friends may not make up for the fact that, if you don't live and work onboard full-time, you'll not only be paying for everything associated with the boat—the boat, the slip, the gas, etc.—but you may also be paying for your life on land. You may still have a mortgage or rent payment due the first of every month, and car and insurance payments. Full-time liveaboards sometimes maintain storage units to stow seasonal gear, collections of prized LPs, and the like. As in all other aspects of onboard living, flexibility and a willingness to simplify will go a long way where your fiscal and mental well-being are concerned.

ALONE AT LAST

You can prepare at least for the expense associated with living and working onboard. It's much harder to prepare for the isolation that can come with the change in lifestyle. In "real life," i.e., when you use your boat exclusively for recreation instead of as a mobile office, everyone wants to come along when you say you're going out on the lake for a cruise. And if you go out alone, you can pretty much count on finding some new friends on the water. But when you make the move to live and work onboard, everything changes, to an extent that can be unsettling.

Some people, Kent Bridges for example, thrive on the isolation. His day job as vice-president of sales for Digital Persona (a biometrics

Liveaboards in cold-water ports lose many of their neighbors come winter.

company) means he spends every working minute with clients, wining and dining, schmoozing and selling, so that when he gets back to his boat, he says, "The privacy is priceless."

Superman had his Fortress of Solitude, where he could go and recharge his inner batteries, so it's only fair that we non-Kryptonians have a similar option. But if your career isn't as intensely public as in sales—writing, for example—the solitude can become overwhelming. To live and work onboard is to remove yourself from society, from your circle of friends, and your normal routine. You also separate yourself from your job and your coworkers even more than when you choose to work from home.

That sense of isolation has a lot to do with the marina you call home. If you're on an inland body of water, you may well be the only person in the marina for many days. Or you may find the only other people in the marina are transient, stopping off for just a night or a weekend, never to return. But other marinas have a different personality. Some liveaboard communities are as strong and welcoming as the most old-fashioned small-town neighborhoods. Kent Doyle says there is more camaraderie at his marina than he experienced in ten years of living in the New York suburbs. Weather permitting, he says, on many evenings the people in the marina congregate on each other's boats, sharing dinners, drinks, friendship, and the day's bluefish catch. Members of the houseboat community in Sausalito, California, report potluck dock parties every month, where everyone brings food and pitches in to serve and clean up. Donna Emmons and fellow liveaboards hang out at a local restaurant famous for live Dixieland music. She says the members of her community respect each other's privacy but are always there to help. It's important to do your research first, sampling different home ports and finally choosing one that meets your need for socialization or privacy.

The Internet is a great outreach resource as well. It has made it a lot easier to hook up and share experiences with others in this lifestyle, and can be a valuable source of anecdotal information from people who've dealt with the same problems and issues you're facing. *Cruising World* magazine's web site (*www.cruisingworld.com*) has a good message board that connects liveaboards around the world in a lively discussion of everything from the best way to paint the bottom of your boat to whether to take your kids onboard for a few years. There's also a very good e-mail list that you can subscribe to (*www.irbs.com/lists/live-aboard*).

E-mail and cell phones help, but most people need a physical connection to other humans. Even Kent Bridges, who sees his solitary

Nature-loving liveaboards can "get away from it all" any time they desire, without even leaving "home."

"Ship Shape"

Getting enough exercise doesn't require a gym membership. It doesn't even require fancy exercise equipment.

A good pair of running shoes costs less than a bike and is safer on ladders.

A set of dumbbells offers a wide range of workout possibilities, whether you're in the marina or out on the water. These AquaBells fill with water—so you can drain them for minimalist storage profile.

Cardio doesn't get much more low-tech than this. Like dumbbells, a jump rope can be used whether you're on land or on deck.

time onboard as a respite from a crazy world, admits that a big reason he eats dinner at the marina restaurant and often hangs around afterward unwinding with a couple of glasses of wine is for the fellowship with other liveaboards.

You can make great friends while living and working onboard, but you have to be in a place and position to do so. If you're going to stay onboard for an extended period, ideally you should pick a home port that actually has a liveaboard community. And even if there's not a big liveaboard community for you to hook up with, you can usually find a nearby restaurant or bar with a crew of regulars who can satisfy your need for real human contact.

Carey and I didn't anticipate isolation being much of a concern. We'd have each other and we'd be close enough to our hometown—less than thirty minutes from downtown, actually—for it to be no trouble to have friends out for a day on the water or for us to drop into town for an afternoon or the movies or whatever. We'd also have the dogs and the cat for company.

"SHIP SHAPE"

A bigger concern was how we and our pets would get our daily dose of exercise. There's nothing very strenuous about operating a twin-engine powerboat equipped with power steering. Besides, I'd been running for more than fifteen years, and I couldn't imagine giving up my daily four-miler with the dogs. I tried to calculate how many laps around the cockpit of the Cobalt 360 would equal one mile but got so dizzy I gave up. And running up and down the floating docks of a marina is a recipe for disaster. So this posed a bit of a problem. I could, in theory, spring for a treadmill, but it would pretty much take up every available inch of room in the cabin. It would also make the potential for motion sickness much greater for Carey and the menagerie because the force of my running would make the boat bob.

For exercise, my friend Suzan Gough swears by t'ai chi, sometimes called Chinese yoga, and swimming. T'ai chi, which can look like slow-motion karate, improves balance, a major bonus for boaters. The stretching movements make the body limber, tone up muscles, and help release tension. On top of that, Suzan calls it one of the best forms of meditation around, ideal for stress relief. Best of all, she points out, it can easily be done on the deck of your boat, a dock, or a beach.

Another option is a folding bicycle, such as the Dahon Mariner 26. Priced around $350 and designed specifically for boaters, the Mariner 26 is a full-size portable bike that folds in seconds to fit easily into any boat hold. Featuring Shimano 21 speed gearing, GripShift shifters, Power V-brakes, and even a suspension seat post, the Mariner 26 is ready to tackle any kind of terrain. Folded, it's only 14" x 27" x 36" (38 x 69 x 91 cm), although the bike's 32.5-pound weight means you probably won't be hauling it around all that easily. A bike like this not only greatly increases your mobility around the docks but makes it easier for you to get some much-needed exercise by going for a ride when the mood hits.

You can buy exercise stands that turn your regular bike, like the Mariner 26, into a stationary bike that can be set up on the deck to get a sweat going when an on-land ride is out of the question. The double-duty aspect is a good thing. For us, an added bonus was the fact that we could take a ride on land and bring the dogs to run along beside us while we biked, enabling everyone to come back to the boat tired and happy.

The same can be said for a good pair of running shoes, and they cost a lot less than a bike. You may not be able to run laps onboard, but you can run anywhere else, with or without canine companions. And I'll say

TIP

If you're going to be using weights of any sort onboard, the smart move is to invest in a 3' x 3' piece of ¾-inch plywood and cover it with indoor/outdoor carpeting to use as your lifting area. Then, if you accidentally drop a dumbbell a little harder than you should, it's most likely going to bounce loudly but harmlessly off the plywood instead of knocking a hole in your boat's deck.

Dahon's Mariner 26 folding bicycle: who needs a roof rack?

A dog to walk or run guarantees at least some exercise every day.

that one of the truly great pleasures in this life is taking a run on a hot summer afternoon that ends with a leap off a dock into the cool water, even if it is in the questionable waters of a marina. Climb up on the foredeck and feel the endorphins course through your brain.

Weight training is possible onboard, too. As long as you're not training for a bodybuilding competition, a pair each of 10-, 20- and 30-pound dumbbells will let you keep firm and trim while taking up a minimum of onboard space. There are even dumbbells on the market that you fill with water and then empty for easier storage.

To sum up, if you're serious about finding ways to work out, you can find them: jumping rope on deck or on the dock, for instance, or doing chin-ups on the radar arch (not recommended by the boat builders but perfectly doable), and push-ups and sit-ups on the foredeck. You can also buy exercise videos or DVDs.

Or you can take the Kent Bridge's attitude. When I asked him about working out onboard, he laughed, saying he gets all the exercise he wants walking to and from the marina's restaurant. (Then he admitted that he gets his real exercise on his Utah horse ranch each weekend.)

FLEXIBILITY IS KEY

Everything in life has costs and comes with challenges. Buy a house and you have to deal with property taxes, insurance, and maintenance. The same goes for your car or truck. You take those costs and challenges into account and see if they outweigh your need and desire for the object. It's hard to argue that anybody actually needs to live and work onboard a boat. But some of us want to, and that should count for something. Whether it counts for enough to overcome the costs and challenges associated with living and working onboard is something we each have to figure out for ourselves. I really wanted, for example, to live and work onboard in a coastal area, but events conspired to make that too expensive for me in terms of what I'd have to give up: my broadcasting job with FOX.

The key is to be flexible, to evaluate the costs and benefits of your decisions constantly, and to remember that no one's forcing you to do anything. If it doesn't work out, it's okay to choose a less-expensive option, or even become a part-timer or a weekender instead of a year-round, full-time liveaboard.

Last, take heart from knowing that some people—especially those willing to simplify dramatically—have found the experience a lot less costlier than others have. In fact, in Tom MacNaughton's words: "Living onboard is a way of life in which an income equivalent to a minimum-wage shore job can allow you to not only live well, but to save money. I know of at least one couple who did mostly odd jobs on boats, repairs and such, and wrote some as they traveled around. They always, no matter how little they made, put a percentage into investments. Now, after about thirty years of sailing around and essentially working whenever they stopped anywhere for any length of time, they're financially independent and need never work again. And they've had an incredibly happy life."

CHAPTER 8

TOGETHERNESS

I'VE ALWAYS BELIEVED THAT EVERYTHING—A GLASS OF IRISH WHISKEY, A SUNSET, OR YOUR WHOLE LIFE—IS SOMEHOW IMPROVED BY SHARING IT WITH SOMEONE IMPORTANT. HAVING SPENT TIME LIVING AND WORKING ONBOARD ALONE AND THEN WITH A PARTNER, I HAVE TO SAY THAT IT'S MUCH, MUCH BETTER TO HAVE SOME COMPANY ONBOARD WITH YOU. THE GOOD TIMES SEEM A BIT BETTER AND THE BAD ONES NOT QUITE SO AWFUL WHEN YOU HAVE SOMEONE ELSE ALONG.

When the idea of embarking upon this lifestyle change for a year took control of my brain, I never thought that Carey wouldn't come along enthusiastically. Luckily, I was right, but that's not something anyone should take for granted. That's why the most important thing you can do, from the minute you start thinking about living and working

CONTENTS

► Compromise

► Family Matters

► Animals Onboard

Taking turns going on shore leaves or exploring will help relieve pressure of too much time together.

onboard, is to talk over the entire matter. Make a compact that every decision will be reached mutually and that you'll each have total veto power. That's a good rule of thumb for living and working together anywhere, but it's particularly important in a place where you'll be experiencing a level of togetherness most people in reality can't imagine. In the confines of a boat, there's no room for simmering grudges. There's literally no getting away from each other. That much proximity means there will be times when the way your partner slurps ever so slightly while drinking coffee will irritate you, and there'll be no escaping it.

Some relationships thrive under these conditions, with partners growing so close that others sometimes say they've "lost themselves." In other words, they've ceased to be individuals and have melded into a single, two-headed unit. Of course, that's not necessarily true. Happy onboard couples don't lose their personalities or individuality any more than members of a football team or a military unit do. They simply become part of something larger than themselves.

Unfortunately, you often don't know what kind of person you are or what kind of relationship you're in until you're onboard and in the middle of a rough patch, literally or figuratively. That's one reason a land-based "shakedown cruise" as described earlier is strongly advised—so you'll find out how well you'll deal with this kind of enforced togetherness.

Even the closest onboard couples need some time to enjoy the boat alone.

The most common problem I've heard discussed occurs when one partner starts putting his or her wants ahead of the other, even to the point of flat-out ignoring the other's feelings. One of you decides he or she is the Captain of the Vessel and becomes a version of Captain Bligh, issuing orders and edicts and generally acting like a jerk. Naturally, the other partner chafes and rebels. Suddenly you're living a real-life Mutiny on the Bounty, bound for an unhappy ending.

Conversely, it's not uncommon for one of you to become overwhelmed by the whole endeavor and curl into a metaphoric fetal position. Again, not the best sign for you, your partner, or your relationship.

COMPROMISE

Even the best liveaboard relationships will hit some rough patches. When that happens, it's a good idea to have some ground rules established so you can both step back and get some fresh air, then come back together and work it out. One liveaboard enthusiast, Bill Dietrich, has a very useful web site (*www.geocities.com/bill_dietrich*). The following tips listed there lay out a solid framework for getting along in a close environment:

▶ **Have small areas of complete ownership by each person: bunk, closet, etc.**

▶ **Respect each person's need for privacy at times: let your partner retire to the forecabin or bow and shut you out for awhile.**

▶ **Escape into a book, TV, radio, or cyberspace.**

▶ **Go swimming, snorkeling, or diving without each other occasionally.**

▶ **Take turns visiting other boats or going on a mini shore leave solo.**

Just getting out of each other's hair for a little while can do the trick. A little privacy was the key to Daisy Garnett's successful transatlantic cruise, when she spent six weeks onboard a 48-foot sailboat with four other people. She told the *New York Times* that not a single argument broke out, not because the crew was a gathering of saints, but because the boat's design gave each of them private space when needed.

If you are both working, that can open a whole other can of worms if you don't have similar work habits. Some people have such diametrically opposed work styles that they can't function in close quarters. Our good

> *Not a single argument broke out, because the boat's design gave us all privacy.*
> —*Daisy Garnett, after a six-week cruise with five people.*

Some galleys, like the one at right, accommodate multiple cooks better than others. In a small galley, like the one at left, one chef at a time may be the limit to avoid stress and tension.

friends David Baker and Melanie Guthrie are a perfect example. David has to have utter silence and an immaculate workspace, while Melanie is a whirlwind who works best with the radio blasting and papers scattered everywhere. He's a classic morning person who rises with the sun and is ready to work the minute his eyes open, while she's a committed night owl who'll stay up watching old movies until dawn. There's no way they could both work onboard without driving each other mad. So they don't even try. Their time on the boat is devoted entirely to pleasure and relaxation.

Carey and I are a bit more compatible in our work styles, and we compromise when there are differences. I work best with the radio playing, so Carey chooses the station. (I'm not picky—I just like the background noise.) And when she needs quiet to take a phone call or work on an important paper, I vacate the area, taking the music with me.

Even the closest couples and families may hit snags when they move onboard. In many cases, these snags can be worked out and you'll be able

Even getting dressed in a small, confined space can cause a strain.

to enjoy a lifetime of success living and working onboard together. We offer a few rules of thumb that have helped us.

First, identify the root of the problem. It may be directly attributable to the boat. If the boat is just too small, for example, that can usually be remedied by getting a bigger one. If you hate the people in your marina, you can find a different home port. You can stay in port more often, or you can do more cruising. You can be more equitable in choosing ports of call, spending time at the helm (or away from it), and doing the everyday chores.

If the problem doesn't lie with the boat but with the lifestyle, it's a different story. For instance, someone is getting claustrophobic to the point he or she can barely go below deck to sleep. Your work habits are incompatible. One of you can't stand staying in one port for more than a few days, and the other is terrified of being out in the open water. You're losing work because your clients are tired of dealing with your spotty replies to e-mails and the difficulty of contacting you (cell service isn't always the greatest on waterways, especially in coastal areas). Even Tom MacNaughton, with his long, successful onboard experience, admits, "It's difficult to work with a client when mail is the only reliable communication medium and a letter may take weeks to get to you"

The younger the child, the easier the adaptation to onboard life.

as is sometimes the case when you're cruising. Of course, Internet access and e-mail help this situation greatly. However, if the problems are falling into any of these areas, you have to reevaluate the endeavor and consider living and working onboard only part-time.

FAMILY MATTERS

As mentioned earlier, everything gets even more complicated if you go from being a couple living and working onboard to being a family in this situation. There are hundreds and hundreds of families who do this successfully and swear it's the best life ever. Tom and Nan MacNaughton, for example, raised their daughter, Heather, onboard and have written eloquently about it on their website (*www.macnaughtongroup.com*). The MacNaughtons believe that raising a child onboard is an unmixed blessing for all concerned. The child sees the world and gets to spend essentially all his or her time surrounded by family.

These are good, valid points. However, it's worth noting that it's one thing to raise a child onboard and something entirely different to move a child onboard from a landlubbing life, especially if the kid's entering the teen years, when he or she will almost surely prefer the company of peers to the company of parents. Younger kids seem to take to the onboard life much more readily. But even they can be less than happy about leaving their friends to spend all their time living on a boat with Mom and Dad. One family at Donna Emmons' marina has found a compromise that works for them. The children are homeschooled onboard, but the parents make a point of involving them in local and public school activities such as sports teams, dancing lessons and school plays. All three children have made close friends in the community.

Remember, too, that kids' minds change at the drop of a hat. The fact that they were excited by moving onboard back when you first brought it up doesn't mean they'll still be excited three days after moving onboard. So be flexible. Don't force things. It's more important to have a strong,

TIP

The Calvert School is a good source of information on home schooling: *home.calvertschool.org* happy relationship with your kids than to live and work on your boat. The boat will be there in twenty years; by then, the kids will most likely be on their own.

According to those who know, babies and toddlers bring different variables to the living and working onboard equation. Babies can do pretty well in a car seat most of the time, and many families report that the gentle rocking has a relaxing effect on infants. Diapers and other necessities, though, can take up lots of space. Disposing of or cleaning diapers is another issue altogether. It's tough to find a diaper service that will follow you from port to port, although you might be able to find one if you stay put. I'm not a parent, but I think I can say with confidence that not even the proudest new Mom or Dad is keen on spending a couple of rainy days in a boat cabin with disposable diapers that have been used but not yet discarded.

Most people I've talked to believe that toddlers can handle living onboard pretty well, although they require almost constant supervision no matter how well the boat has been baby-proofed. However, toddlers are considered more or less insurmountable obstacles when it comes to working onboard.

ANIMAL LOGIC

I admit to no personal experience with babies or toddlers onboard, but I do have some experience with pets. Carey and I love our pets. Mali, Curtis Ray, Baby Lucy, and Tutu have been by our sides virtually every day of their lives. The three dogs lounge with us, exercise with us, even sleep with us. (Tutu, the cat, tends to be a little more solitary, but we still love him.) Some find this a little overboard (pun intended), but we're far from alone. Kent Doyle shares his boat with his ex-wife's two dogs, a Maltese and a Maltese-Shih Tzu cross, which he admits are small, white, and fluffy. "No real man would like these dogs," he told the *New York Times*, "but they ended up loving me, and I love them inordinately."

Almost all dogs take to boating naturally, although you do have to make some accommodations. According to Dr. Rick Lusk, DVM, of the Westgate Pet and Bird Hospital in Austin, Texas, the most important thing to remember is that dogs are more susceptible to heat and dehydration than we may realize. "Heat's probably more dangerous than anything else," Lusk says, "and it's especially dangerous for puppies, older dogs and little dogs." Dogs regulate their core temperatures through panting, so it's important to provide lots of cool water. It's also important to provide some shade where the dogs can lie down and enjoy the cool breeze away from the sun.

Dogs may be natural swimmers, but they don't really float very well, especially heavily muscled breeds like Rottweilers. Personal flotation devices (PFDs) should be required wearing any time your dogs are on the water. Ruff Wear (*www.ruffwear.com*) makes K-9 Float Coats, PFDs that are designed to float the dog in a natural swimming position and have extra-strength handles to help you give them a lift when it's needed.

There are a couple of other reasons for having your dogs wear PFDs. First, those grab handles make it easier to help your dog back into the boat when he jumps for a swim. Although most dogs are great jumpers and swimmers, and even pretty good climbers, they're helpless if their back feet can't find footing. This is why dogs will often swim right up to a swim platform, get their front paws up, and then start to flail helplessly, getting more and more panicked. With the PFD, you can give your dog the tug he needs to get up into the boat. The other benefit is that the PFD lets the dog swim with even less effort, so he'll be less likely to wear himself out, something that Dr. Lusk says is a real concern.

"Dogs will overexert themselves if you're not careful," he says, and anyone who's spent six hours playing fetch with a Labrador retriever knows that's no lie. "So it's up to you to monitor the activity level. Try to stick to fifteen-to-twenty minute periods of activity followed by rest."

Like certain people, some dogs are victims of motion sickness. If your beloved golden retriever can't make it around the block in your Suburban without tossing his Milk Bones, then it's a pretty safe bet that he's not going to do too well on a boat. But that's not to say he can't come along for the fun. According to Dr. Lusk, dogs, like people, respond well to Dramamine. Emetrol may work, too. (Our dogs don't suffer from motion sickness on boats, so we've never had to test these products.) Consult with your vet before heading out for an extended cruise to see what dosage would be appropriate for your four-legged friends. Even if

> 66Dogs will overexert themselves if you're not careful.99
>
> —*Dr. Rick Lusk, veterinarian*

your dogs aren't terribly bothered by motion sickness, it's a good idea to limit feeding before and during your on-water adventure, opting instead for a big meal when you get home. Some large-breed dogs are susceptible to bloat (gastric dilation volvulus, or GDV), which is life-threatening, so one hard and fast rule is to enforce a one-hour rest period before and after eating.

Dogs of all sizes don't understand the concept of bracing themselves, so letting your dogs roam loose while the boat's under way isn't a good idea. And even though they love getting up in the bow and sticking their faces in the wind, they should never ride up front. If you hit a wake your dog can be thrown out of the boat. There are harnesses you can use in the car or truck to secure your dogs, but none of them have been successfully adapted for boats. Probably the best thing you can do when you're under way is to leash the dog and have him sit or lie next to you. He'll still get plenty of excitement and wind, but he'll be much safer.

The K-9 Float Coat has a sturdy handle on the back, so you can help haul your animal out of the water safely.

TIP

Introduce pets to boating by spending a little time onboard without going anywhere. Turn on the engines to let them become accustomed to the unfamiliar noise.

Ruff Wear's Bark 'N Boots are also required gear to keep the dogs' nails from shredding your boat's upholstery and scratching the daylights out of the deck. It's a rare dog that likes them at first wearing, but they provide some serious benefits. The Bark 'N Boots have soles made from Reprotek (recycled tire rubber), which gives your dog better footing and traction, especially on an uncarpeted deck.

Dogs need exercise, especially if they're young. Most dogs enjoy swimming, but they also need to run and play, two things that aren't always easy to do on a boat. Carey and I take daily runs with our three dogs, something we've done since they were pups. Kent Doyle has a dog walker come by daily to exercise his two dogs. Also, dogs eat a lot, and what goes in must come out. When it does, you have to deal with it.

Cats eat, too, but their bodily functions are a little easier to deal with, requiring only a litter box that's cleaned out regularly. It's even possible, with patience and determination, to train your cat to use the head. (We haven't.)

Cats make great onboard companions. They can be completely content lounging around the clock, so you don't have the exercise hassles you have with dogs. In many cases, the only concern you'll have with a cat is making sure it has a scratching post to keep its claws short and sharp (otherwise it'll use whatever's handy, including your boat's upholstery). Cats need their claws for protection, so a declawed cat is a helpless cat. Declawing shouldn't be an option. If your cat's claws are a problem, despite having a scratching post, you can trim them with regular toenail clippers.

Believe it or not, cats are pretty good swimmers when they have to be. Only rarely will they actively seek out the opportunity to dive in, however. Many dogs, on the other hand, will go barreling into the water at every chance. So when we're under way, we have an onboard policy in which Tutu (our cat) stays in the cabin with the door closed and the dogs are leashed so they can't jump off. Any time we're stopped and the dogs are in the water, the engine is turned off and the keys are removed from the ignition for safety. Dogs are pretty smart, but they don't understand the potential dangers of a propeller.

A couple of items that should always be onboard if you have pets are Ruff Wear's Traveler First-Aid Kit and the book *Pet First Aid: Quick Guide to Animal Emergencies*, also available from Ruff Wear.

As important as it is to have a good first-aid kit onboard for yourself, you also need to make sure you're properly prepared in case your pet requires medical attention. Whether or not you get your animal first-aid kit from Ruff Wear, you would do well to follow its lead:

▶ **A copy of *Pet First Aid* (see above)**
▶ **Four 3" x 3" gauze pads**
▶ **Two 5" x 9" trauma pads**
▶ **Two lengths 4" x 4.1 yd. stretch gauze**
▶ **One 2" x 5 yd. cohesive flexible bandage**
▶ **One pair latex gloves**
▶ **One pair metal scissors**
▶ **One plastic forceps**
▶ **One 3 oz. bottle iodine**
▶ **One 4 oz. bottle eye-skin wash**
▶ **Two insect swabs**
▶ **Two 1 g. tube hydrocortisone cream**
▶ **One 1 oz. tube antibiotic cream**
▶ **Five cotton swabs**
▶ **Two antiseptic towelettes**
▶ **One powdered styptic**
▶ **Two soap towelettes**
▶ **One handiwipe**
▶ **One laminated Gunshot Wound Card**
▶ **One spool 2" x 5 yd. adhesive tape**
▶ **One 8" x 10" resealable bag**
▶ **One pencil**

ANIMALS ABROAD

If you're living and working in a coastal area and may be traveling to another country, you'll need to do some research on the legality of bringing your pets along. It's usually not a big deal.

To bring dogs or cats into Mexico, all you need is a certificate stating that your pet has been vaccinated against rabies, hepatitis, pip, and leptospirosis, and an official health certificate that must be issued by a veterinarian no more than seventy-two hours before entering Mexico. There is no quarantine period for bringing a pet into Mexico, and you can bring up to two large pets (dogs or cats). Any more pets require permission, easily obtained from your nearest Mexican consulate.

Cats and dogs older than eight months may enter Canada from the United States if accompanied by a certificate of an official government veterinarian. There is no quarantine period and no limit on size or number of pets, within reason.

The Bahamas are a popular destination for those based in Florida, as they are only a day away. An import permit is required from the Ministry of Agriculture, Trade and Industry (Nassau) for all animals being brought into the Commonwealth of The Bahamas. Applications for such permits (along with a ten-dollar processing fee) must be made in writing to the Director of Agriculture, Ministry of Agriculture, Trade and Industry, P.O. Box N-3704, Nassau, The Bahamas. (For more information, call 242-325-7502 or 325-7509.) The animal must be six months of age or older. The animal must also be accompanied by a valid certificate that states the pet has been vaccinated against rabies within not less than one month and not more than ten months prior to importation. And the animal must have a Veterinary Health Certificate, which must be presented within forty-eight hours of arrival in the Commonwealth of The Bahamas to a licensed veterinarian for an examination.

CHAPTER 9

CHARTING YOUR OWN COURSE

IF YOU ASK ANYBODY WHO'S DONE IT, LIVING AND WORKING ONBOARD A BOAT IS ONE OF THE MOST REWARDING EXPERIENCES ONE CAN HAVE. A MAJOR PART OF THE REWARD IS OVERCOMING ALL THE OBSTACLES. THERE ARE TIMES WHEN IT SEEMS LIKE THE FATES ARE COMPLETELY AGAINST YOU, THROWING UP ONE HURDLE AFTER ANOTHER AND DOING EVERYTHING IMAGINABLE TO MAKE YOUR LIFE UTTERLY MISERABLE. BUT AFTER ALL THE MISGIVINGS, THE WORK AND PREPARATIONS HAVE PAID OFF, AND YOU EXPERIENCE THAT MOMENT WHEN THE UNIVERSE SEEMS TO WORK PERFECTLY AND ALL YOU HAVE TO DO IS ENJOY IT: THE FREEDOM, THE PEACE, THE BEAUTY OF THE MARINE ENVIRONMENT, AND THE EXCITEMENT OF DOING SOMETHING DIFFERENT.

Those who've successfully made the transition have some things in common. To begin with, they wanted it to work. Secondly, they went into the project with

CONTENTS

▶ Making It Work
▶ Our Floating Office
▶ Our New Routine
▶ Flexibility

It's not all smooth sailing, but living and working onboard a boat can be uniquely rewarding. Those who've done it successfully have a lot in common, including wanting it to work in the first place.

Unlike home ownership, living aboard gives you the freedom to move whenever you want.

their eyes open. The dream of a carefree life like the kind Jimmy Buffet sings about, in which you drink margaritas all day while deciding which fabulously exotic port you'll visit next, is just that—a dream. And if you think that's what you're getting into, you're in for a rude awakening.

If you go into it cautiously, however, pondering all the realities and your own particular situation, there's no reason you can't live and work onboard very successfully for as long as you want to stay on the water. Marinas from Portland, Maine, to Portland, Oregon, are filled with people doing just that.

On The Liveaboard List, a private message board on the Internet, Jeff Smith wrote a brilliant summation of why many live and work onboard. "I have always been independent of spirit," he wrote, "believing that only I know what is best for me, and further believing that I can live with my mistakes much better than I can live with the mistakes I make when forced to act by someone else's rules. I don't like being told what to do, or how to think. I sense that most liveaboards are similar in nature.

"It seems to me that living aboard offers more freedom to be who you want to be. If you want a powerboat or sailboat it's your choice, and generally no one is going to knock you for the choice you make. In fact, I have found the opposite to be true. In most cases boaters tend to be supportive of their differences. Aside from the gentle teasing that we both enjoy, I've never encountered any real sail vs. power animosity.

"And another thing. If you don't like where you are, the rules there, the government, your neighbor's dog, or your neighbor for that matter, you can up and move. Try that with a house.

"To me, the whole liveaboard attitude isn't really about living on a boat, it's about community. It's not about where you live, or what you live in, or what you live on. Power, sail, trawler, multi, mono, whatever, you are still a part of your community, doing it your own unique way. That's the freedom I crave and another one of the reasons that I moved aboard."

KEEP YOUR COOL

Another characteristic of those who make a successful go of living onboard is flexibility when it comes to dealing with contingencies. Nothing throws them. Engine trouble means learning how to fix it. A money shortage means finding a quick part-time job to bring in some cash to keep things afloat. They never see a setback as anything but temporary. In another life, they'd be the sort of obnoxious optimists who keep saying, "When one door closes, another opens." If you can embrace this mindset, you can succeed, too.

Humor is critical. If you can't laugh at yourself for forgetting to put oil in the engine you just had rebuilt, thereby ruining it (this really happened to someone I know; I promised to keep his name a secret), then you won't make it on the water.

I don't know if it comes from a combination of optimistic flexibility and a great sense of humor or from somewhere else entirely, but everyone I know who's living and working onboard has this almost inexplicable faith that everything will work out—and that if it doesn't, it really doesn't matter in the big scheme of things. Such a mindset is about the most soulful way of living I've ever encountered. I'm sure spending time out on a pitch black body of water with the stars visible over the horizon gives you a peculiar perspective on your place and importance in the universe, and every successful liveaboard shares it.

Of course, sometimes perspective is hard-earned. There's a learning

> "Living aboard offers more freedom to be who you want to be."
> —*Jeff Smith*

curve for any new enterprise. Decisions must be made and mistakes must be learned from—or avoided. One of the better decisions we made was to spend some time "sampling" marinas for a night or two before settling on a home port. It's a strategy that should work in coastal areas and on lakes as well. A marina has a personality, just like a neighborhood, and you can't really get a feel for that personality until you've been there for a few nights. If you're someone who values peace and quiet, you don't want to discover that the marina bar or restaurant becomes party-central every Thursday through Sunday night. And you won't know that if you only drop by for a quick visit on a Tuesday afternoon.

The home port Carey and I chose was a full-service marina that was attached to the Lakeway Inn Conference Resort, a complex with lots of amenities: a hotel, five golf courses, tennis courts, pools, a restaurant, and a couple of bars. Over the years, I had often used Lakeway as a base of operations when doing boat tests for magazines. As a result, I had developed strong professional relationships with Lakeway's management team, both at the resort and the marina. These relationships, along with our familiarity with and love of the resort, put Lakeway ahead of the competition from the beginning. As an added bonus, with five golf courses minutes away from the marina, I could dash over for a round of golf or at least a practice session at one of the driving ranges anytime I had a break from a deadline. In addition, there was the allure of having the Travis Bar only a short walk from the boat, so Carey and I could always choose to end our day with a cocktail overlooking the water.

The place was super-convenient and ideal for us. I was particularly happy with the marina's excellent security systems. Security can be a concern for liveaboards. Even though boats come with locks on the doors, in warm weather you want to keep things open. That can make your boat a target for burglary or vandalism. With all that expensive electronic equipment onboard, it was comforting to see Lakeway's security guards patrolling the resort, including the entrance to the marina, in their golf carts. That's something I wasn't as aware of as a visitor to the place as I became when we were actually living there. So we made a good decision to sample before choosing a home port.

HIDDEN AWAY

Another good decision was going wireless. Wireless connectivity let us use the entire boat, making the prospect of spending serious time onboard much more enticing. It also helped eliminate clutter. The AirPort relies on radio frequencies, instead of the infrared light of old-school remote devices. Radio waves, unlike infrared light, can pass through walls and windows. You don't need to have line-of-sight access from a remote device to a base station to make things work. So we were able to hide virtually everything we weren't using out of sight and out of our way, again helping to increase the effective space onboard. The AirPort and printer/scanner shared closet space in the main cabin. All I had to do was drill a hole in the closet using a half-inch bit so that the power cords from the AirPort and the printer/scanner could reach the electrical outlets. You wouldn't even know those two crucial pieces of equipment were onboard.

Secreting those two items in the closet also helped protect them from any possibility of water damage. Even in the roughest water or a driving rain, the closet remained bone-dry, so it was also the logical space for us to stow our computers when they weren't in use. Again, the power cords could pass through that half-inch hole I'd drilled in the closet. With the closet door latched and the computers in their carrying cases, our Macs were probably safer from inadvertent moisture damage, even on a boat, than if they were sitting on a landside desk with a cup of coffee only inches from the keyboard. (I should mention, though, that this solution might not be safe for year-round liveaboards in cold climates, since most closets are not heated. Donna Emmons recalls finding a sweater frozen to the outside closet wall one February morning.)

Carey Kelley, working from the V-berth.

> We had a fully functional mobile office that you couldn't even see.

TIP

Use self-adhesive stamps onboard. Lick-and-stick stamps will fuse into a useless blob.

Done right, it turns out you don't need all that much physical space to fully equip an office. By eliminating unnecessary items and forcing everything to pull at least double duty, Carey and I were able to have a fully functioning mobile office that you couldn't even see if we had the computers stowed in the closet along with the AirPort and the printer/scanner. The V-berth was our communal desk, the mid-cabin berth our slacker palace, the cockpit our conference room, and our workstations were wherever we and our computers happened to be at the moment. Our cell phones rode along in our pockets or sat beside us as we worked. If you saw us from shore or from another boat, you'd never have thought we were working. Even if you came onboard you'd probably have been surprised to find how productive we were.

Keeping the place as uncluttered as possible helped. Old salts will tell you that it doesn't take long on the water for you to learn what you really need and how to jettison the rest. Over the course of a career in journalism, I had come to believe that in order to do my job I needed at least a dozen spiral notebooks nearby at all times, a few dozen of my favorite ballpoint pens, and reams and reams of paper for the fax machine and printer. I also had thought I needed a storage shed full of files, some dating back to my very first assignment as a writer (just in case I ever needed to look something up) and a full library at my fingertips, at least in part because being surrounded by books and written material somehow made me feel more like a writer.

Carey was more flexible. When I'd get ready to go restock office supplies, I'd ask her what she needed and she'd invariably say, "I'll just use some of yours." And she did. Which should have given me the hint that I really didn't need as much stuff as I had thought.

Looking at the Cobalt's storage spaces, I realized I'd have to learn to get by on next to nothing compared to what I'd become accustomed to. Carey and I agreed that we would assign one drawer for office supplies. If they couldn't fit in that drawer, we didn't need them. We'd have probably been a bit more generous with the supply space if we'd been going coastal, where we might be more than a quick jaunt from the local Office Depot. But because we were on an inland lake with all kinds of access to a semi-major city, we figured we could make resupply trips as needed.

SAVED BY—AND ON—THE CD

Then we decided to try not to make any resupply trips at all, in spite of the fact that most of us in the working world generate paperwork as effortlessly and voluminously as we generate carbon dioxide. It's easy to fall into the habit of first getting or putting everything in writing and then hanging on to that writing forever. So even with mountains of blank papers and acres of filing cabinets on hand, we're always finding ourselves needing more of each. It doesn't have to be that way. By getting rid of the fax machine and saving the faxes received by our computers digitally, we cut down on both paper use and file space. By scanning all nonlegal documents and saving them digitally—and recycling the paper—we saved even more filing-dedicated space. Invoicing, which had previously been done by printing an invoice, faxing it to the client, filing it until paid, and then filing both check stub and paid invoice, became a matter of generating a digital invoice on the computer, faxing it from the computer, scanning the check upon arrival, linking that file with the

A printer or fax is workable onboard when you're docked, but all equipment must be stored when under way.

TIP

Use CDs as file folders to cut storage space to a bare minimum.

invoice, and saving the linked files to a CD. This soon gets you to a point where about the only things you're printing out and saving are legal documents, which can be filed in a waterproof plastic bin, or better yet, sent to someone on shore for safekeeping.

Living an almost paper-free life means a single ream of blank paper will last for weeks, so you only need to buy a ream at a time. The same goes for printer ink: virtually no printing means you don't have to keep spare ink cartridges around.

We were able to reduce our office supply stockpile to a single ream of paper, a stapler, a tape dispenser, a box of paper clips, a box each of large and small binder clips, a box of envelopes, and a couple of sheets of stamps—the self-adhesive kind, because lick-and-sticks will inevitably soak up enough humidity to glue themselves together into a useless blob. We also kept a stack of fifty CD-RWs, a pair of scissors, four spiral notebooks, and two dozen ball-point pens. The whole shebang fit into a single drawer with room to spare. We even used the same drawer as a temporary filing area to hold legal papers until we could get them sent to our attorney for safekeeping.

Cutting everything down to the bare essentials like that didn't have nearly the adverse impact you might think. It takes a while to get used to scanning and saving every piece of paper that comes across the transom, and it's odd at first to send and receive documents that never physically exist. Once it's a habit, though, it's incredibly liberating not to have to shuffle through stacks of paper to find what you're after.

The system that worked best for us was the one that used the CDs as miniature file folders. One CD, for example, held all the documentation regarding the boat (all the hard paperwork was held by our attorney). Another CD held all our bills, which we'd scan and annotate with the date and amount paid as well as method of payment. Since virtually every aspect of banking can now be done on-line, we almost never wrote a check or mailed a bill. Just point, click, and pay. Each project we worked on had its own CD. Because each CD can hold so much information, it's possible to go a year or two using fewer than fifty CDs, which take up hardly any space.

Generally, our office functioned well. We quickly fell into a comfortable routine. For the first few days we followed the daily to-do list. It was a pain at first, but following the list made sure that we never forgot or overlooked anything. After a few days, it became second nature and we didn't even think about it.

A NEW ROUTINE

Usually we'd wake up early, in tandem with the sun. That was when the dogs would also wake up and let us know they were ready to go outside. One of us would leash the dogs and take them for a morning walk up the docks to a grassy area, while the other would start coffee and begin running through the morning checklist.

One of the major highlights of our day was deciding how we'd exercise the dogs, because that was a great way to break up the daily routine of work. Some days we'd stay docked and take the dogs for a run. Other days we'd ride our bikes while the dogs ran alongside us. The best days, though, were when we'd motor out to a secluded cove where a friend gave us access to his anchor buoy. We'd tie up and spend the day alternating between sessions of working and swimming. Those were the days when the lifestyle seemed to be everything we'd ever dreamed it would be.

But at the end of even the most enjoyable day, we needed to eat, and cooking dinner could be a challenge. Either Carey or I would take the dogs for a long evening walk while the other would prepare dinner, relatively unmolested by creature companions. (Tutu often hopped up onto the counters, but at only seven pounds he was easily brushed back down.) However, it only took a couple of attempts at fixing an elaborate dinner for us to embrace Tom MacNaughton's simplicity ethos when it came to cooking. The Five Ingredient Rule was invoked. (No dish should have more than five ingredients, including spices.) One-pot or one-skillet dishes were the entrees of choice, because they meant less to clean up.

One-pot cooking with only five ingredients stretches your culinary skills. Those skills are stretched further if you follow a vegetarian diet, as we did. We found stir-frys to be the easiest dishes to cook, although a second pot is required if you're going to have rice. We ate a lot of stir-frys. We also ate a lot of tacos, using meat substitutes instead of ground round.

But despite the expense, the allure of dining at a waterside

> *The Five-Ingredient Rule: no dish should have more than five ingredients, including spices.*
> *—Tom and Nan MacNaughton*

restaurant where we wouldn't have to do the cooking or cleaning was often irresistible, especially if we'd fixed anything more exotic than cold cheese sandwiches for lunch. (Breakfast was rarely anything more involved than a grapefruit and toast, so it wasn't a big deal.) Our galley gear was sufficient for cooking and dining, especially considering our conscious choice to prepare meals as simply as possible. As long as there was just one of us in the galley, there was enough room to cook comfortably. However, if the dogs were onboard, getting excited by the smells and activity of cooking, it could seem as though we were trying to cook in a broom closet. So we ate out more than we had planned.

GOING TO THE DOGS

Cooking with the animals underfoot was a breeze, though, compared to working. Within a couple of weeks, it became clear that it was going to be a constant challenge to get much work done with all those animals onboard. Space, feeding (it's easy to forget to leave room for the dog food bin), and exercising all became serious concerns. Shedding was also a tremendous problem. It seemed at times that Carey and I were spending more time vacuuming up animal hair from the cabin and cockpit than doing anything else. Dog and cat hair was on our computer keyboards, our sheets, our countertops, and everywhere else, no matter how hard we worked to keep it under control. We had overlooked the fact that in the summer even shorthaired dogs shed.

During our "shakedown cruise," shedding didn't seem to be a problem, maybe because we cheated more than we realized and let the dogs outside frequently. More likely, shedding was less of a problem then because the dogs were much less stressed in our house than on the boat, and stressed dogs are heavy shedders.

Finally, there was the issue of the poop patrol, as we came to call it. On land, when the dogs needed or wanted out, we opened the back door and off they went, into the yard, until they were ready to come back in. On the boat, though, when the dogs needed out, we had to leash them up and take them, usually all three as a pack. We weren't as strict about the leashes as we should've been during the shakedown cruise, so the reality of going for frequent walks didn't sink in until we were onboard. Carey kept telling me that she'd heard it was possible to train dogs to use a litter box, but that was an even less appealing thought than the frequent walks. We already had one litter box onboard. Two was more than I could bear to imagine in such close, and often closed, quarters.

PERFECT DAYS, BUT...

We didn't have a problem supporting our work activities from onboard—at least not technically and logistically. Carey used her cell phone constantly, conducting her animal rescue work—calling shelters to see whether any Catahoulas had turned up and then trying to place the dogs with foster owners. It was easy for me to set up my TV pieces from

> ❝ To live and work onboard is to choose a simpler life. ❞
> —*Tom MacNaughton*

The mid-berth on a Cobalt 360 is comfortable but snug.

the boat, and since what I was covering was likely to be shot outdoors, I didn't have to dress up like an anchorman. The khakis and polo shirts I had brought were perfectly adequate. We kept a car at Lakeway, and I would commute to locations and then to the studio for editing.

So on the face of it, there was really no reason this lifestyle shouldn't have worked for us. But it takes a lot of discipline to work at home; and it takes exponentially more to work on a boat when the sun's high and the water's calm, and all you really want to do is motor out or swim.

We forced ourselves to knuckle down, but both of us began to have a few doubts about living and working onboard full-time—at least on a boat of the size we had chosen—for a whole year.

TERRA FIRMA

As Randy Harmon writes in an excellent SailNet piece (available on-line at *www.sailnet.com/collections/cruising/index.cfm?articleid=harman0013*), "Sooner or later, the cruising must come to an end for all of us." In talking to those who've tried living full-time aboard and decided to return to the landlubber life, I've found that there's rarely one identifiable reason for moving back. In fact, I've only heard of one case in which people moved back to land for one specific reason: A couple ended their liveaboard experience when the wife got pregnant and flat-out refused to raise her child anywhere else but on terra firma. Fair enough.

Tom McConnell's message on The Liveaboard List is fairly typical of the reasons people leave the liveaboard lifestyle. "My wife and I sold our boat last fall and moved back to land," he wrote. "It was both one of the hardest decisions we've made and one of the easiest. I had lived aboard for five years, and after we married, Rachel and I lived aboard for eight months. Last summer the marina changed owners and the slip fees doubled—thus easing the decision to sell—although there were other concerns like commuting, space on the boat with two of us, etc."

Carey and I had grown accustomed to having a certain level of comfort and technology in our lives, and we'd gone to great lengths to try and maintain those levels when we moved onboard. That was unrealistic. Given the size of our boat and the needs of our human and creature family, we couldn't duplicate that level of comfort without living far beyond our means. As Tom MacNaughton had told me again and again, to live aboard is to choose a simpler life, and we hadn't done that.

Another thing we hadn't done was lessen our workloads to accommodate our new lifestyle, because we weren't in a financial position to do so. All of my professional activities and most of Carey's were conducted onboard, and trying to meet deadlines week after week in the boat's cramped quarters was a major source of stress, even with the best-working equipment.

Others who work and live onboard, like Kent Doyle, Donna Emmons, and Kent Bridges, either have landside "day" jobs or can do much or most of their work in clients' offices. Their boats are used more as backup offices

On a boat of this size, there's plenty of room to work and relax.

Living and working onboard successfully means charting a course that suits your own financial, personal, and professional needs.

than as a primary work space—a place to tackle a few hours of work every now and then or complete an intensive, short-term project. Boaters who are semiretired, or can afford to work only a day or two every few weeks would be in the same position, which seems ideal to me.

But we were not in that ideal position.

After several months, we came to realize that the kind of boat we liked, at the size we could afford, wasn't adequate for full-time onboard living for an extended period of time. So we sold the Cobalt (at a loss, as expected) and moved back on land.

Although we no longer have the Cobalt, we still live and work onboard borrowed boats for short periods of time, several times a year. We do still have the office equipment. On the one hand it makes for a great home office. On the other hand, when we manage to arrange a boat for a few weeks up in Vancouver, or for a month in Rockport, we're able to easily pack up our computers and AirPort, as well as our XM boom box and cell phones, and take our office with us. (We don't travel with the printer/scanner/copier.) We book the dogs and the cat into a kennel, pack up our mobile office, and we're off. Since we know it's only for a little while, it's that much easier to find in ourselves the things that make living and working onboard a success—flexibility, humor, and a sense of our real place in the universe. And when it's time to pack up and come home, we do.

That's the magic word: FLEXIBILITY. Boaters have to adapt to the constraints of their lifestyle, and that requires making some sacrifices and changing some expectations. But we're also free to choose among countless variations of the onboard life: it can be as mobile (or not) and as spacious (or not) and as tied to the land (or not) as you like. When you find the proper combination, you're golden.

ACKNOWLEDGMENTS

The author acknowledges and thanks Laura Kelley, Tom Gonter, Joe Skorupa, Matt Trulio, Tom and Nan MacNaughton, Kent Bridges, Donna Emmons, and Kent Doyle for their support, encouragement and assistance over the course of this project. Without them, this book could not have been written.

The publisher wishes to thank the many manufacturers and suppliers of products and services for their generous assistance. Please see Resources, page 173, for contact information.

PHOTOGRAPHY CREDITS

Cover, half-title page, 13, 28, 58, 80, 87, 144, 146 (left), 174: Courtesy Beneteau USA; Table of Contents, 17, 26, 29, 30, 32, 33, 35, 36, 44 (bottom), 102, 148, 155, 169: Courtesy Sea Ray; Page 8: Corbis; Pages 10, 34, 92, 104, 130: Photodisc; Page 11: Courtesy Sooke Harbour House; Pages 12 (Luhrs M400), 40 (Hunter 426), 84 (Luhrs S43), 95 (Luhrs M430), 124 (Luhrs S43), 142 (Luhrs M430), 182 (Hunter 456): Courtesy Luhrs Marine Group; Pages 15, 52 (top), 116 (left), 138 (bottom), 140: Photospin; Pages 18, 24, 62, 75, 96, 98, 146 (right), 181: Courtesy Island Packet Yachts; Pages 19, 91 (right), 117: NOAA; Pages 22, 116, 176: Courtesy Viking Yachts; Pages 38 (top), 71, 85, 163: Andrew Willett; Pages 38 (bottom), 39, 120, 137, 171: © Neil Rabinowitz; Pages 44 (top), 61, 132, 167: Courtesy Cobalt Boats, Inc.; Pages 50, 91 (left and center), 99, 106: Ablestock; Page 52 (bottom): Clipart; Page 53: Marge Beaver, Photography-plus. www.photography-plus.com; Pages 54, 56, 133, 136, 156, 158: Skip Hubbard Photography; Pages 64, 82, 147, 161: Robert Pressley; Page 67: Courtesy KVH, Inc.; Page 68: Todd Cooper; Pages 110, 111: Courtesy West Marine; Pages 114, 125, 126: Courtesy BoatU.S. Marine Insurance; Page 129: Courtesy Sea Tow Services International, Inc.; Page 138 (top): Aquabells Travel Weights; Page 139: Dahon California, Inc.; Page 151: © Ruff Wear. www.ruffwear.com

RESOURCES

Websites

Clothing and Gear
www.westmarine.com
www.landsend.com

Destinations
www.sookeharbourhouse.com

Food and Meal Planning
www.mealtime.org

Fractional Ownership
www.psboats.com
www.fractionalyachts.com

Homeschooling
home.calvertschool.org

Internet
www.kvh.com
www.apple.com (AirPort)
www.dlink.com

Laptop Computers
www.dell.com
www.apple.com/powerbook

Liveaboard Communities
www.irbs.com/lists/live-aboard
www.cruisingworld.com
(message board)
www.geocities.com/bill_dietrich

Marinas
www.betweenthebridges.com
www.pilotspoint.com
www.lakewaymarina.com

Marine Insurance and Assistance
www.boatus.com
www.seatow.com

Mobile Phones and Wireless Service
www.nokia.com
www.motorola.com
www.kvh.com

Online Boat Shopping
www.marinemax.com
www.boats.com
www.nadaguides.com

Pet Products
www.ruffwear.com

Powerboats and Cruisers
www.carveryachts.com
www.cobaltboats.com
www.luhrs.com
www.searay.com

Printers
www.epson.com

Recreational Equipment
www.aquabells.com
www.dahon.com

Safety and Safe Boating
www.uscgboating.org
www.redcross.com

Sailboats
www.beneteauusa.com
www.islandpacket.com
www.huntermarine.com

Satellite Radio
www.xm.com
www.sirius.com

Satellite Television
www.dishnetwork.com
www.directv.com
www.KVH.com

Trawlers
www.nordictug.com

Weather Information
www.weather.com
www.weather.gov
www.noaa.gov

Weather Software
www.weatherbug.com (PC)
www.afterten.com
(WeathermanX, Macintosh)

Books

Brewer, Ted. *Understanding Boat Design* (4th Edition). Camden: International Marine/Ragged Mountain Press, 1993.

Maloney, Elbert. *Chapman's Piloting and Seamanship* (64th Edition). New York: Hearst Books, 2003.

Sargeant, Frank. *The Complete Idiot's Guide to Boating and Sailing.* (2nd Edition). Indianapolis: Alpha Books, 2002.

Teale, John. *How to Design a Boat* (2nd Edition). Dobbs Ferry: Sheridan House, 1997.

INDEX

A

accidents, 125–28

accommodations. *See berths; cabins; galleys; heads*

aesthetics, 45

After Ten software, 91

age of liveaboards, 20

air conditioning, 94

AirPort technology, 62–63, 69, 76, 161

amplitude modulation (AM) radio, 70

anchoring, 123–24

animals, 166–67. *See also pets*

The Arizona Republic, 36

Austin, Texas, 42, 86–87

automobiles, 168

B

babies, 149. *See also children and boating*

Bahamas, 154

Baker, David, 146

banking, 164

barbecue grills, 134

barges, 37, 68

Bark 'N Boots, 152

barometric pressure, 93

Basic Boat Saver Policy, 125

bathrooms. *See heads*

batteries, 82

bedrooms, 31

Beneteau boats, 28

berths, 27, 161, 162

Forward berth on a Beneteau 393.

bicycles, 130, 139

Big Red, 54

bilge pump, 103

bilge storage, 101

bill payment, 164

Black & Decker Dustbuster, 80

bloat (gastric dilation volvulus), 151

Blue Book (NADA), 43, 46

Bluetooth technology, 62

boat comparisons, 23–45

boat design/architecture, 25

boat-handling skills, 16, 29, 107–8.
    See also safety

boat selection, 23–45

Boat Town, 42, 56, 74

Boatsafe.com, 15, 16

Boats.com, 41

BoatU.S. insurance, 125

books. *See resources and references*

boundaries, 96. *See also privacy*

Brewer, Ted, 25

bridge-design boats, 32, 34

bridges, 57

Bridges, Deb, 54

Bridges, Kent

    on exercise, 140

    on food preparation, 134

    home port, 54

    on installing electronics, 74

    on office space, 76

    on routines, 100

    on solitude, 135–36, 138

    on space issues, 78

    on wardrobe, 88

    on work schedules, 169

brownies, 98

buoys, 118–19

C

cabins, 61, 167

Calvert School, 148

camaraderie of liveaboards, 136–38

can buoys, 118

Canada, 154

capsizing, 111

captains, professional, 35

carbon monoxide poisoning, 36–37

career/work, 13, 20, 55–56. *See also offices on*
    boats; work routines; work space

cats, 152. *See also pets*

CDs and CD players, 62, 63, 71, 163–64

cedar chips, 96, 98

cell phones. *See mobile phones*

challenges of living on board, 131–41

channel markers, 116–18, 117, 118–19

Chapman, Charles Frederic, 15–16

Chapman Piloting (Maloney),
    13, 15–16, 173

chartering boats, 47, 48

charts, 30, 116, 119, 122

checklists

    checks and tests, 115

    daily routine, 102–3

    float plans, 108–10

    home port selection, 53

kitchen gear, 97

office equipment, 60, 81, 164

pet first-aid kits, 146–47

predeparture checklist, 113–15

systems checks, 115

wardrobe, 83, 87–88

children and boating, 148

boating classes, 16

diaper services, 149

flotation devices, 111

Internet resources, 148

privacy needs, 19–20

teens, 148

very young children, 33, 149

choosing boats, 23–45

claustrophobia, 147

cleanliness and organization

adjusting to onboard living, 94, 95–99

animal shedding, 166–67

cabin, 95

Claustrophobia is less likely on this spacious Viking V581S than on smaller boats.

Dustbuster vacuum, 80
galley, 103, 132, 133–34
odors, 96, 101–2
office organization, 164
routines, 99–100
septic system, 101–2
wireless networking, 161
closet space. *See storage space*
clothing/wardrobe
checklist, 83–85, 87–88
closet space, 84–85
dressing space, 147
mildew protection, 98
minimalist wardrobe, 78
multiple-use wardrobe, 85–86
seasonal variations, 88
weather and, 86, 87–88, 89, 110
work clothes, 167–68
cloud types, 91, 91–93, 92
clutter, 95–98
Coast Guard. *See U.S. Coast Guard*
Cobalt 360
cabin, 61
cruising, 45
draft, 116, 121
galley, 132
midberth area, 132
prices, 45–46
salon, 44
storage space, 84, 162
TV/VCR combo, 167
cockpits, 32
coffeemakers, 77

comforts of houses, 168–69
common sense, 17
Commonwealth of the Bahamas, 154
communications, 13, 19, 144. *See also*
    mobile phones
community of liveaboards, 37, 136–38, 159
commuting, 168
comparing boat types, 23–45
compatibility, 146–47
The Complete Idiot's Guide to Boating and
    Sailing (Sargeant), 15, 173
compromise, 145–46
computers. *See also Internet connection; wireless*
    technology
daily routines, 102–5
electricity source, 62–63, 64–65
laptops, 13, 71, 80
moisture protection, 64, 64–66, 79, 161
office peripherals, 60
PC equivalents, 65
storage/protecting, 79–81
contingencies, 159
convenience, 52
cooking. *See food preparation; galleys*
copiers, 60, 65
costs of boats and living aboard, 25, 33, 131,
    132, 141
couples boating
boat size and, 28, 29–32
boating safety and, 17
children and, 18–21
decision-making process, 45–46
staterooms, 31

work styles, 63

CPR class, 112

crew, 18–21

cruising, extended, 27–28

cruising insurance extensions, 127

cruising range, 31

Cruising World, 137

cumulus clouds, 91, 92

cycling, 130, 139

D

Dahl's porpoises, 12

Dahon Mariner 26 bicycle, 139, 139

damage to boats, 111, 125

dealers, 42

"death zone," 36–37

decision-making process, 9–21, 45–46, 144

Delphi SkyFi receiver, 72

depth sounders, 30, 116, 119

design of boats. *See boat design/architecture*

desks, 62, 75, 76, 161, 162

diaper services, 149

diesel fuel, 42, 45

Dietrich, Bill, 145

Digital Persona, 136

digital storage, 163–64

dining, 54, 133, 165

DirecTV, 67, 69, 90

discipline, 168

Dish Network, 67, 90

distress calls, 112

dogs, 140, 165, 166–67

Doyle, Kent

  background, 52

  boat heaters, 94

  on camaraderie, 136–38

  formal clothes, 86

  office, 71

  pets, 149, 152

  on self-sufficiency, 73

  storage options, 84, 85, 88

  trawler, 32, 38

  on work schedules, 169

draft of boats, 30, 115–16

Dramamine, 104, 150

drinking water, 99, 100–101, 102

DSL, 67. *See also Internet connection*

duct tape, 64

dumbbells, 134, 138

Dustbuster vacuum, 80

DVDs and DVD players, 19, 62, 63, 135

E

education, 33, 148. *See also safety*

elderly boaters, 20

electronic position indicating radio beacon (EPIRB), 111

electronics and electrical systems. *See also computers; wireless technology*

  anchor lights, 124

  batteries, 80

  CDs and CD players, 62, 63, 71, 164

  electronic storage, 163–64

  entertainment, 19

importance of, 46–47

installation, 72–75, 78

new and used boats compared, 37–39

office power, 60–61, 64–65

shore power, 47, 56, 94, 102

e-mail, 137. *See also Internet connection*

emergencies. *See also safety*

emergency kits, 111, 113

preparing for, 110–11

procedures, 112, 113

Quick Guide to Animal Emergencies, 153

towing insurance, 128

Emetrol, 150

Emmons, Donna, 161, 169

employers, 9

engines, 31, 37–39, 94

entertainment. *See also Internet connection*

cost, 134–35

DVDs and DVD players, 19, 62, 63, 135

personal computers, 63–64

radio, 70–72

salon room, 29

television, 69–70

TV/VCR combo, 167

EPIRB (Electronic Position Indicating Radio Beacon), 111

Epson Stylus CX5200, 65

etiquette in boating, 24

exercise

clothing, 85–86

cycling, 130, 139

gear, 134, 138

options, 138–40

pets, 140, 152

expense of living on board, 25, 33, 131, 132, 141

experience in boating, 14

explosions, 111–12

Express Bridge, 32, 34

F

family and boating, 17, 142. *See also children and boating*

boat size, 33–34

living aboard, 11

port selection, 52–53

privacy needs, 18–21

stress management, 13

towing boats, 43

fans, 94

faxes, 60, 65, 163

FedEx, 53, 133

fellowship of liveaboards, 37, 136–38, 159

fiberglass, 40

filtration systems, 101

finances, 20, 141, 159, 164

fire extinguishers, 111, 112

fire procedures, 112

fires, 111–12, 114

first-aid kits, 111, 153

fishing boats, 22

Five Ingredient Rule, 165

flare guns, 111, 112

Flatley, Dan, 98

Flatley, Sharon, 98

flexibility, 13, 141, 149, 159, 170

float plans, 103, 108–11

flotation, 89, 110, 111, 150. *See also
personal flotation devices (PFDs)*

FM (frequency modulation) radio, 70

folding bicycles, 139

food preparation. *See also galleys*

   brownies, 98

   canned goods, 101

   coffeemakers, 77

   groceries, 133

   kitchen gear, 97–98

   refrigeration, 77, 103, 105

   routines, 102–5, 133–34

   simplicity, 97–98, 165–66

forks in waterways, 118–19

foul-weather gear, 86, 110

fractional ownership, 47–48, 170

Fractional Yachts Inc., 48

freedom of living on board, 158

frequency modulation (FM), 70

freshwater, 99, 100–101, 102

fuel, 31, 42, 43–45, 127, 132

G

galleys. *See also food preparation*

   Cobalt 360, 132

   coffeemakers, 77

   daily routine, 102

   kitchen gear, 97–98

   midcabin galley, 32

   on sailboats, 28

   on Sundancer boats, 31

   types of, 146

   variety of, 146

Garnett, Daisy, 69, 145

gas grills, 134

gasoline, 42, 45

gastric dilation volvulus (GDV), 151

Gauguin, Paul, 10

generators, 47, 94

getaways, 11–12

ginger ale, 104

Gough, Susan, 138–39

GPIRB (Global Position Indicating
Radio Beacon), 111, 112

GPS (global positioning systems), 111, 112

grills, 134

groceries, 133

grounding, 121, 122

guests, 32, 97

Gulf of Mexico, 11, 30, 43, 51

gust fronts, 93

Guthrie, Melanie, 146

H

habits. *See routines*

Harmon, Randy, 168

heads, 98. *See also septic systems*

health certificates, 154

health issues, 17, 103–4, 111, 112, 149–52,
152–54. *See also safety*

heaters, 94

Highland Lakes, 11

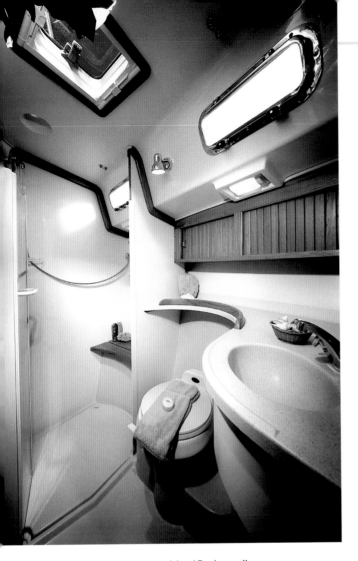

The forward head on an Island Packet sailboat.

hit-and-run accidents, 127

Holland, Michigan, 34

home port, 51–57, 147

homeschooling, 33, 148

houseboats, 36–37, 137

How to Design a Boat (Teale), 25, 173

humor, 159

Husted, Jerry, 37–39

I

installations, professional, 74–76

installing electronics, 72–75, 78

insurance, 125–28

international travel, 153–54

Internet connection

    boat-office checklist, 60

    e-mail, 137

    intermittent service, 148

    marina rules, 53

    satellite phones and, 66, 67–68

    wireless, 66–69

Internet resources

    on boat manufacturers, 25

    boating safety resources, 16

    Boatsafe.com, 15, 16

    Boats.com, 41

    BoatU.S. insurance, 125

    liveaboard resources, 32–33, 137, 148, 158, 168

    MarineMax.com, 41

    Mealtime.org, 103

    SailNet, 168

    U.S. Coast Guard, 109, 116–19

    weather forecasts, 90–91

Intracoastal Waterway (ICW), 118–19

IRBS liveaboard list, 78

Iridium satellite phone service, 66

isolation, 135–38, 147

J

jump ropes, 138, 140

K

K-9 Float Coats, 150, 151

Katadyn Micropur Forte Water Preservative, 101

Kelley, Carey, 82, 161

Kelley, Dave, 82

kitchen. *See galleys*

KVH satellite telephones, 67

KVH TracVision C3, 69

L

Lake Austin, 116

Lake Lanier, 43

lake levels, 122

Lake Travis

    author's time on, 158

    channel markers, 118–19

    as home port, 43, 55, 56

    insurance requirements for, 128

    level fluctuations, 119

    weather, 90

lakes. *See* specific lakes

Lakeway Inn Conference Resort, 160

Lakeway, Texas, 56

land-based storage, 88

laptop computers, 13, 71, 80. *See also computers*

This Hunter sailboat has a length overall (LOA) of over 45 feet.

large boats, 35, 35

laundromats, 97, 98

laws pertaining to boats

    insurance requirements, 125–27

    owner responsibilities, 39

personal flotation devices (PFDs), 110

safety equipment, 110–11, 113

leaks, 111

leasing boats, 47–48

legal documents, 164

length overall (LOA), 26

life rings, 112

lifestyle issues, 53, 135–38

lightning, 92

litter boxes, 167

The Liveaboard List, 158, 168

living space, 25, 33. *See also salons*

Lusk, Rick, 149–50

M

MacNaughton, Heather, 148

MacNaughton, Nan, 32, 52, 141, 148

MacNaughton, Tom

    background, 52

    on family boating, 32, 148

    on food preparation, 97–98

    on perspective, 105

    on simplicity, 69, 165, 168

    on working on board, 147

mail service, 53, 54, 56, 132–33

maintenance

    boating education and, 16

    daily routines, 102–5

    handheld vacuums, 80

    new and used boats compared, 37–39

    sanitation, 99–100

Maloney, Elbert S., 15–16

Manatee (trawler), 32, 52

Manhattan Island, 34

marinas, 51

    camaraderie, 136–38

    electrical hookups, 56

    facilities, 53

    fees, 54, 168

    home ports, 160

    Old Saybrook, Connecticut, 55

    personalities, 136–37, 147, 152

    restaurants, 133, 134

    security, 160

    selecting home port, 51–57

    solitude, 136

    urban access, 52, 53

marine assistance coverage, 128.

    See also insurance

marine wildlife, 10, 12, 13

MarineMax.com, 41

McCammon, Jane, 36–37

McConnell, Tom, 168

Mealtime.org, 103

medical issues, 17, 111, 112, 149–52, 156

Mexico, 154

Miami, Florida, 88

midberth area, 132

midcabin galley, 32

mildew protection, 98

mobile phones

    advantages, 162, 167

    costs, 134

    coverage, 53

    remote work, 10, 13

service, 66, 147

modems, 60, 65. *See also Internet connection*

moisture protection, 64–66, 96, 98, 161

mold, 98

Morse code, 119

motion sickness, 103–4, 150–51

motor trim, 121

motor yachts, 32, 34, 35

Motorola T721 phones, 66, 69

movies/videos, 134–35

music, 63, 70–72

N

National Automobile Dealers Association (NADA), 46

National Institute for Occupational Safety and Health, 36

National Oceanic and Atmospheric Administration (NOAA), 90

National Weather Service, 91

nautical charts, 30, 116, 119, 122

navigation, 116–19, 120, 121

navigator's desk, 62

neap tides, 122

neatness. *See cleanliness and organization*

new boats, 37–39, 131

New York City, 34

The New York Times, 149

nimbus clouds, 91, 92

Nordic Tug, 37

nun buoys, 118

O

odors, 96, 101–2

offices on boats, 59–81. *See also work space*
  shown, 58
  on barges, 68
  boat size and, 25
  choosing a boat, 24
  copiers, 60, 65
  desks, 62, 75, 76, 161, 162
  DSL, 67
  faxes, 60, 65, 163
  home-office test, 77–79
  Kent Doyle's office, 71
  office layout, 163
  office supplies, 60, 163–64
  printers, 60, 65
  wireless technology, 161–62
  work styles, 63

Old Saybrook, Connecticut, 55

one-pot cooking, 165

optimism, 159

orcas, 10, 12, 13

organization. *See cleanliness and organization*

ownership, fractional, 47–48, 170

P

Pacific coast, 30

Pacific Northwest, 10

paper-free living, 163–64

parking, 53

personal flotation devices (PFDs), 17, 110, 111, 112, 150

personal relationships, 143–49

perspective, 105, 159–60

Pete's Harbor, 54, 100, 134

Pet First Aid: Quick Guide to Animal Emergencies, 153

pets

exercise, 138–39, 140, 165

first aid, 153

litter boxes, 167

as liveaboard companions, 149–54, 170

marina rules, 53

shedding, 166

Pettengill, Ann, 39

PFDs. *See personal flotation devices (PFDs)*

pickup trucks, 43

pontoon boats, 36–37

porpoises, 12

postal service, 53, 54, 56, 132–33, 163

power boats, 22, 23–24, 159. *See also specific boats*

Powerbook, 62

prices of boats, 25, 34, 41, 45–46

printers, 60, 65

privacy, 19–20, 34, 144, 145, 147

property taxes, 34

Puget Sound, 11

purification systems, 99–100

R

radio, 19, 70–72, 90, 111, 135

rain gear, 86, 89, 110

ranges of boats, 31

Raven, Clayton, 42, 56, 74

Red Cross CPR class, 112

Redwood City, California, 54

refrigeration, 77, 103, 105

relationships, 143–49

renting boats, 47–48

resale values, 45–46, 69

research, 41

resources and references. *See also Internet resources*

Blue book (NADA), 43

Boating for Dummies, 15

boating skills, 15–16

Chapman Piloting (Maloney), 14, 15–16, 173

The Complete Idiot's Guide to Boating and Sailing (Sargeant), 15, 173

Cruising World, 137

How to Design a Boat (Teale), 25, 173

Soundings, 37

Understanding Boat Design (Brewer), 25, 173

restaurants, 54, 133, 165

retirement, 20, 170

retrofitting, 47

rewards of living on board, 157–70

Rockport, Texas, 51, 55

rode (anchor line), 123

The salon of a Carver 570.

routines. *See also checklists*

    adjusting to life onboard, 83–105

    animals and, 165

    checklists, 102–5

    office matters, 164

    required safety checks, 113–15

    systems checks, 115

Ruff Wear, 150, 153

running, 139

S

safety, 107–28

    anchoring, 123–24

    basics, 16–18

    boat draft, 115–16

    boat size, 29–30

    boating safety courses, 15–16, 127

    carbon monoxide poisoning, 36–37

    CPR class, 112

crew safety, 18–19

distress calls, 112

draft of boats, 30

drinking water, 99, 100–101, 102

fire extinguishers, 111, 112

fire procedures, 112

first-aid kits, 111, 153

float plans, 103, 108–11

forks in waterways, 118–19

grounding, 121, 122

hit-and-run accidents, 127

marina security, 160

navigating shallows, 121

personal floatation devices (PFDs), 17, 110, 111, 112, 150

predeparture checklist, 113–15

safety kits, 112

signs and markers, 116–19

storms, 89–94

swimming, 15, 17, 152

systems checks, 115

tides, 122

towing, 126

water purification, 100–101

Weather Channel, The, 72

Sail & Ski, 42

sailboats

  clearance for masts, 57

  cruising speed, 42

  galley, 28

  as offices, 24

  powerboats compared with, 23–24

SailNet, 168

salons, 29, 34, 35

saltwater environments, 101

San Francisco Bay, 54, 88

San Juan Islands, 13

sanitation systems, 98, 100, 103. *See also septic systems*

satellite technology, 53, 66–68, 71–72

Sausalito, California, 37, 137

scanners, 65

schooling, 33

Sea Ray boats. *See also Sundancer boats*

  cockpit, 32

  as example fleet, 25

  prices, 41

  salon, 44

  Sport Yachts, 31

Sea Tow, 128, 129

seamanship, 14, 16, 20, 29, 107–28

seasickness, 98, 103–4, 150–51

seasonal weather changes, 88, 94

Seattle, Washington, 43

seaworthiness, 27–28

security, 14, 160

sedan bridges, 32, 35

self-adhesive stamps, 163, 164

self-sufficiency, 73, 158

septic systems, 98, 100, 103

"shakedown cruises", 77–79, 144–45, 166

shallows, 120, 121

shopping, 41–42, 133

shore power, 47, 94

shortwave radio, 70

signs and markers, 116–19

simplicity, 69–70, 97–98

Sirius radio, 71, 135

size of boats

    couples boating, 28–32

    draft, 115–16

    family and, 33–34

    living aboard, 170

    office space, 24–25

    safety, 29–30

    for solo liveaboards, 26–28

    towing, 43

    weather and climate, 27–28

    work styles and, 147

skills for boating. *See seamanship*

sleeping quarters. *See berths*

Smith, Jeff, 159

solitude, 10, 17, 53, 135–38

solo boating, 17, 20

Sooke Harbour, British Columbia, 11, 13

Soundings, 37

South Austin Marine, 42

space constraints. *See offices on boats;*
   storage space

Sport Boats (Sea Ray), 31

spouses, 45–46. *See also couples boating*

spring tides, 122

spring weather, 94

squalls, 89

stamps, 163, 164

staterooms, 31, 33, 34

stationary bikes, 139

storage space

    bedroom, 84

    bilge, 101

    on Cobalt 360, 84

    design variations, 32–34

    galleys, 102

    home contrasted with boat, 78

    land-based, 88

    office equipment, 75, 162

    for shoes, 85

    solo liveaboards, 27

storms, 89–94

Strait of Juan de Fuca, 11

stratus clouds, 91, 92

strength of boats, 37–39

stress management, 12–14

sun protection, 85–86

Sun Sport yachts, 35

Sundancer boats. *See also Sea Ray boats*

    accommodations, 26

    cockpit, 32

    couple-sized, 29–32

    design variations, 32–34

    family-sized, 32, 33

    large yachts, 35

    prices, 41

    salon, 44

    selling points, 46

    stateroom, 44

sunsets, 104

swamping, 111

swimming

    cats, 152

    daily routine, 165

    as entertainment, 135, 158

The television is mounted on the master stateroom wall in this Luhr M400.

as exercise, 138, 140

safety, 15, 17

systems checks, 115

T

Tahiti, 10

t'ai chi, 138–39

tape decks, 71

taxes, 34

Teale, John, 25

technology, 13, 46, 167. *See also computers;*
   wireless technology

teens, 148. *See also children and boating*

telephone service, 53, 54, 60, 66, 137–38. *See also*
   mobile phones

television, 19, 69–70, 90–91, 167

temperature, 85–86, 93, 94, 149–50

Texas Hill Country, 11

Thoreau, Henry David, 10, 11

thunderstorms, 92. *See also weather/climate*

tides, 116, 122

toddlers, 149. *See also children and boating*

togetherness, 143–54

toilet. *See heads*

Total Protection Yacht Policy, 125

TowBoatU.S., 128

towing, 27, 30–31, 43, 126, 128, 129

TracNet 2.0, 67–68

Tracphone 252, 66, 67

TracVision, 74

transatlantic voyages, 69, 145

transition to living on board, 157–58

transportation. *See towing*

Traveler First Aid Kit (Ruff Wear), 153

traveling routine, 103

Travis Bar, 160

trawlers, 32, 37–39, 161, 162

tug boats, 37–39

Twain, Mark, 88

U

Understanding Boat Design (Brewer), 25, 173

uninsured boater coverage, 127

United Parcel Service (UPS), 53, 133

urban marinas, 52, 53

U.S. Coast Guard

boating safety courses, 15

fire procedures, 112

float plans, 108–10

navigation rules, 116–19

Power Squadron, 16

predeparture checklist, 113–15

used boats, 29, 40–41, 131

V

V-berths, 27, 161, 162

vaccinations, 153–54

vacuums, 166

Vancouver Island, 11, 13

ventilation, 94

VHF (very high frequency) radio, 111

video games, 19

Viking 61, 22

voice mail, 10. *See also mobile phones; telephone service*

W

wardrobe. *See clothing/wardrobe*

warranties, 42

Wasilewski, Stan, 78

waste systems. *See septic systems*

water, drinking, 99, 100–101, 102

water damage protection, 64–66, 96, 98, 161

water levels, 119. *See also tides*

Waterfront Restaurant, 54, 134

Weather Channel, The, 90–91

weather/climate, 19

boat size and, 27–28

clothing requirements, 85–88

cloud types, 91, 92

daily routines, 102–5

family considerations, 21

foul-weather gear, 86

lightning, 92

seasonal changes, 88, 94

storms, 89–94

temperature, 85–86, 93, 94, 149–50

weather forecasts, 90–91, 93, 103

weather radios, 90

WeatherBug, 91

WeatherManX, 91

websites. *See Internet resources*

weekend trips, 9–10

weight loss, 17–18

weight training, 138, 139, 140

"welcome home" buoys, 119

West Marine, 89

WiFi Internet access, 69

wildlife, marine, 10, 12, 13

wind, 92–93

wireless technology

    advantages, 161

networking, 62–63

office neatness and, 75–76

remote work, 9

satellite connection, 67–68

Windows-based, 65

work routines, 13, 14, 63, 145–46, 168–69

work space, 59–81, 146. *See also offices*
   on boats

X

XM radio, 71, 72, 135